CANADA

Contents

Irving Weisdorf & Co. Ltd.

C ANADA IS A COUNTRY THAT DEFIES AN EFFORTLESS OR elementary description. It is diverse in its geography, climate, economy, wildlife, and fittingly, in its people. The country's contrasts are beautiful ones, providing variety, mystery and challenge for all who reside in and visit this great land.

The country's motto, 'From Sea to Sea,' could be a way of saying it has everything in between. Massive mountains … wide, golden prairies … fierce rock, sculpturesque ice, dense forest, indomitable wilderness, sophisticated cities, farmland, parkland, valleys, rivers, lakes, oceans, arctic tundra, sand dunes … all of this and more is Canada. Canadians can brush shoulders with hundreds of people in an afternoon or spend days away from civilization. They experience harsh winters, sweltering summers and live across six time zones in the world's second-largest country. There are two official languages in Canada – English and French – but many more are spoken. Possibly the widest variety of people in the world, with their many races and religions, call Canada home – creating a mosaic of colourful customs and character.

So named by the Huron-Iroquois people, 'Canada' originates from *Kanata* which means village – a fitting name considering the sense of home Canadians share. Amid the contrasting and diverse elements of this country there is a constant component – exquisite beauty. Simply put, the sun sets each night on a truly beautiful scene, anywhere in Canada.

LAND OF THE WILD, LAND OF THE FREE AND THE land of much geography; Canada is many things. Depending on where one lives or visits, it is a rocky country, a forested region, hilly and flat all in one. Canada is a land of variety substantially because of its enormity.

Many people are surprised to learn that Canada is second in land area only to Russia – it is almost as big as all of Europe combined. This may be difficult to believe because Canada's population is far from the top of the list. A relatively small population of just over 30 million lives in a land that covers 9,970,610 square kilometres. No wonder Canadians project a sense of community and belonging. But the Canadian people are not alone in this huge land – they share their lives with the wilds of nature. About 25 per cent of the country is covered in forest, among other unbridled examples of nature.

Canada's motto, while proud and individual, is not geographically correct, since the country is bordered by three oceans: The Pacific in the west, the Atlantic in the east and the Arctic in the north. Canada's coastline is the longest of any country in the world. This water theme does not end here. Canada's countless rivers and lakes make up approximately one seventh of the world's fresh water – the most of any country in the world. This country contains three of the world's longest rivers and shares seven of the world's largest lakes, the Great Lakes, with its American neighbours.

There are seven geographic regions in Canada. The Arctic Region, in the far north, is an area with year-round ice and snow. In fact, the northernmost part of this region is made up of islands that are frozen together by pack ice for most of the year. This is a land, north of anything 'civilized,' that is both harsh and beautiful. The Mountain, or Western Cordillera, Region includes the Yukon, British Columbia and parts of Alberta. These mountain ranges are one of Canada's most impressive physical features. Amid a huge ice field in the southwest corner of the Yukon Territory, Mount Logan marks the highest point in Canada at 5,951 metres. The region itself is by far the country's most varied and scenic. With plateaus, gorges, hills and river deltas, this area is reaching for the sky and dipping into lush valleys all at once.

The Great Plains is a vast, flat region with fields of wheat and canola growing as far as the eye can see. The desert-like conditions in parts of this region result in sandy winds and rocky waters. These elements have uncovered some of the largest concentrations of dinosaur fossils in the world. Parts of Alberta, Saskatchewan and Manitoba are included in this region of open skies and long, faraway horizons. Above the Great Plains is the Hudson Bay and Arctic Lowlands Region. Not many people reside or visit here. It is a mainly flat, boggy area. The remaining northern part of the country, including northern Manitoba, Ontario and Quebec, west to the northern edge of Alberta and east to Labrador, is the famous Canadian Shield. Wrapped around Hudson Bay, this is Canada's largest geographic feature and is considered the foundation of the North American continent. The granite rock found here is 3.5 billion years old. This is truly an ancient region, scraped by the advance and retreat of glaciers, which left only a thin layer of soil to support a grand boreal forest.

Aged, rocky, rugged and glacially sanded, this region is known for its mining and logging.

In contrast, the area below the Canadian Sheild, known as Central Canada or the St. Lawrence-Great Lakes Lowland, is relatively flat and fertile. Originally farmland and forest, today this region includes the country's largest towns and cities, which are home to half the country's population. Moving east, the final area is known as the Appalachian Region. This hilly and wooded land includes the part of Quebec south of the St. Lawrence River, and all of the eastern provinces. The gently rolling landscape turns rugged toward a deeply indented coastline. A beautiful and tranquil region of Canada, this area is alive with smaller towns and cities and promotes a life influenced by the Atlantic waters.

Each region of this fundamentally disparate country is important to its overall character and identity. Appreciated and celebrated, Canada's geographic differences are fitting in such a vast, great land.

LONG BEFORE THE WELL-DOCUMENTED ARRIVAL OF European explorers such as Columbus, Cartier and Cabot, Canada's true founders were already here – the Native Indians. Ironically, we know them as Indians only because Columbus, when he sailed to America in 1492, thought he'd reached the Indies of Asia so he, of course, called the people he found here Indians. They called themselves, in their own languages, 'the people.' These people, who fall generally into two main linguistic groups, were the Algonquin and the Iroquoi and were part of a larger group that spread across all the Americas from what is now northern Canada far down to the southern tips of present day Argentina and Chile.

The Canadian Indian tribes evolved immeasurably during prehistoric times. The earliest known occupation site in the country is the Bluefish Caves of the Yukon. When the Europeans arrived, in the early 1500s, the Native Indians were well established and not far behind the explorers in terms of technology. The Natives, spread across Canada, had successfully developed a wide range of languages, laws and government. They had well-defined religious beliefs, trading processes, customs, skills, arts, crafts and survival techniques.

Sadly, by both intentional and inadvertent means, the explorers and pioneers brought about an end to the Natives' original way of life. Through disease, battles, land losses, near extinction of the buffalo and a long history of conflict and complication, European discovery is estimated to have reduced the Native Indian population by more than two thirds. The Inuit, or Eskimos, who arrived from Asia after the forebears of all other American Indians, were the last group to give up their traditional way of life. However, partly because of their location in the Arctic, the Inuit remain primarily hunters although they now use more modern housing.

Today, long after the many explorations and battles that took place; after fur-trading, railway building and the formation of the Hudson's Bay Company, political issues involving the Native Indians remain. Although strongly in the public consciousness, the contentious issues of treaties, land claims and rights are not as clearly understood by current Canadians as they could be. In a modern and developed country, many residents lack the knowledge of traditional Native cultures and the modern situations that bring about these tensions.

Still, however and whenever the conflict might end, the Native Indians were indeed the first peoples of Canada, hence the fairly recent and rightful preference for refering to Native Indians as First Nations.

It was on July 1, 1867, that Britain's North American colonies joined together under the terms of the British North America Act to become the Dominion of Canada. The original provinces were Ontario, Quebec, Nova Scotia and New Brunswick. Manitoba entered Confederation in 1870, British Columbia in 1871, Prince Edward Island in 1873, Saskatchewan and Alberta in 1905 and Newfoundland in 1949.

The Yukon Territory was created in 1898, the Northwest Territories in 1905, and Nunavut Territory in 1999.

Even a country as young as Canada has seen war. It was in Ypres, Belgium, in 1915 that Canadian troops saw battle for the first time in World War I. Major John McCrae, from Guelph, Ontario, was an artillery brigade surgeon during the second battle of Ypres. This 16-day battle took the lives of more than 6,000 Canadians. The day after laying friend Lieutenant Alex Helmer of Ottawa to rest, McCrae jotted down a poem on a page he tore from a dispatch pad. This poem is an internationally recognized and momentous reminder of the days of war. It is a result of this Canadian creativity that we wear poppies on Remembrance Day today.

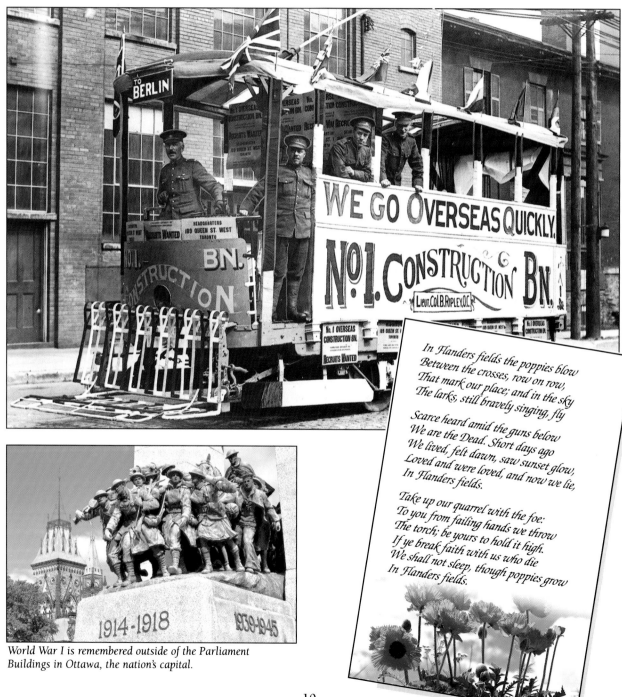

World War I is remembered outside of the Parliament Buildings in Ottawa, the nation's capital.

In Flanders fields the poppies blow
Between the crosses, row on row,
That mark our place; and in the sky
The larks, still bravely singing, fly

Scarce heard amid the guns below
We are the Dead. Short days ago
We lived, felt dawn, saw sunset glow,
Loved and were loved, and now we lie,
In Flanders fields.

Take up our quarrel with the foe:
To you from failing hands we throw
The torch; be yours to hold it high.
If ye break faith with us who die
We shall not sleep, though poppies grow
In Flanders fields.

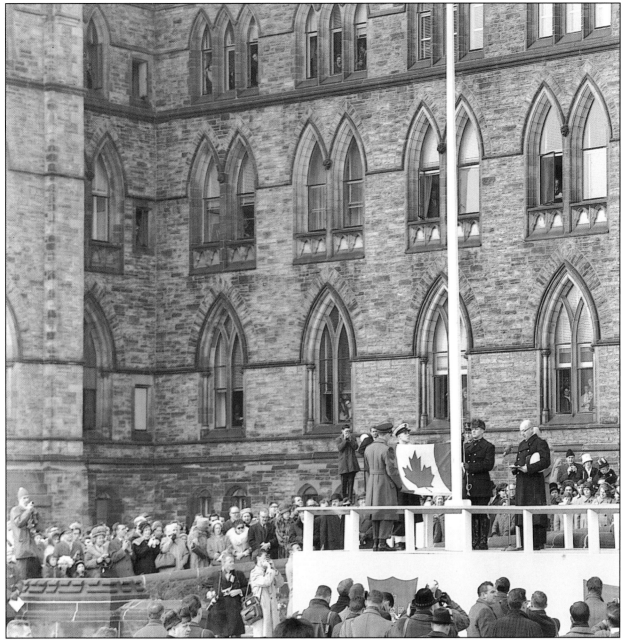

The new flag ceremony takes place on Parliament Hill in Ottawa, February 15, 1965.

The present-day flag of Canada was proclaimed by Parliament on February 15, 1965, after the merits of 2,000 entries were debated. The red side bars represent the ocean boundaries and the maple leaf is the country's floral emblem. The colour blue was avoided on the flag in order to show independence from Britain and France.

Sir John Alexander Macdonald, considered the Father of Canada, was the first prime minister of the country, from 1867 to 1873. During that time he orchestrated the realization of Confederation. He was also an important and responsible figure in the purchase of the western territories from the Hudson's Bay Company, in founding Manitoba and British Columbia and in the vital construction of the Canadian Pacific Railway, which linked Canada from sea to sea.

Sir John A. Macdonald was the first prime minister of Canada.

❧ WORLD-RENOWNED ATTRACTIONS

THE FIRST WRITTEN DESCRIPTION OF **NIAGARA FALLS** was given in 1683 by Father Louis Hennepin, a Recollet priest from the Spanish Netherlands. His account described "an incredible Cataract or Waterfall, which has no equal." His words still hold true today. A small town in Ontario features the world's most popular waterfall. Canada's number-one tourist attraction, and one of the top destinations in the world, Niagara Falls draws 12 million people annually.

This natural and awe-inspiring attraction is approximately 15,000 years old. The Falls span the Niagara River between Ontario and upper New York State, measuring almost 800 metres wide. The vigorous, rushing waters are plunging from Lake Erie toward Lake Ontario, generating a powerful four million kilowatts of energy per second. But it is not the statistics, the measurements or the history of the Falls that interest most visitors – it's their immaculate beauty.

The beauty is not reserved for the summer months only. The winter months offer an equally spectacular view, with the edges of the Falls frozen and parts of the rushing movement hidden behind a magical layer of diamond-like ice. It's not very often that Niagara Falls stop falling, but once, on Easter Sunday morning in 1848, they did stop completely. This caused many people to declare the end of the world. Others decided to scavenge the river bed beneath. As strange as it was, the world was not ending; there was a complicated ice jam cutting off the flow of water to the dropping point.

There have been a number of strange events surrounding the Falls, namely the stunts and daredevilish acts that have been performed there over the years. The first of these was carried out by a French tightrope walker known as The Great Blondin. The first of his many performances was recorded in 1859 as he walked across the Falls on a high wire. The first person to successfully

go over the Falls was an unlikely candidate. A middle-aged school teacher named Annie Taylor hoped to make money by travelling over the Falls in a specially made barrel. She and her cat, which accompanied her, survived the bumpy trip, but she achieved only fame for her efforts. Many people have both successfully and tragically challenged the mighty Falls since then.

Thankfully, most visitors are satisfied with a trip aboard the *Maid of the Mist*. They line up to don hooded ponchos and wait to board the tour boat for a mini cruise to the base of the smaller American Bridal Veil Falls and then to the basin of the magnificent Horseshoe Falls. The experience is both wet and exhilarating. While the natural beauty and wonder of Niagara Falls triumphs over commercialism, the attractions on nearby Clifton Hill are part of the fun-filled experience of the visit. In a carnival-like atmosphere, spots such as Ripley's Believe It or Not Museum and the Criminal's Hall of Fame draw crowds who like a strange tale or two.

There are many popular museums, restaurants, bars and, of course, hotels. Niagara Falls is, after all, the honeymoon capital of Canada and maybe the world. Rumours of heart-shaped beds and hot tubs and the beauty of the Falls themselves have drawn newlyweds here for decades. The latest man-made attraction in Niagara Falls is Casino Niagara. With 2,700 slot machines, 144 gaming tables, blackjack, poker, baccarat and roulette, there's plenty of ways to double your money or just have some fun. The casino also features a variety of comfortable dining establishments and several beverage bars.

Niagara Falls is a thrilling place. But the biggest thrill is the feel of the spray on your face and the thunder in your chest from the world's most magical falls. The world's love affair with this natural beauty is one that will surely never die.

The world's highest free-standing structure can be seen from miles around and enjoyed at the lakefront of the country's largest city, Toronto, Ontario. Reaching 553 metres into the sky, the **CN Tower** has been a favourite destination and landmark for tourists and locals alike since its completion in 1975. The "CN" stands for the builders of this magnificent monster, the Canadian National railway and communications company. Today it's owned by Canada Lands Company, along with a number of other real estate properties. The tower's primary function is communication, transmitting Canada's radio and television signals.

Not only is the tower useful, but it has a unique beauty and is a proud landmark. It is a pleasure to recognize how 106,000 tons of concrete and 4,000 tons of steel can evoke such charm and character. And not only is it a wonder to see, but it provides an astounding view. People from all around the world have taken the 58-second journey in the glass-faced elevators (on the outside of the structure) up to the Sky Pod for a 360-degree view of Toronto and beyond. The Sky Pod is the world's highest observation gallery at 447 metres; from here, on a clear day visitors can see 120 kilometres. An evening view is equally stunning, with a multitude of city lights between the blackness of Lake Ontario and the night sky.

There have been many additions and renovations at the famous tower over the years. Among the most popular is the glass floor. Located on the outdoor Observation Level, this transparent flooring, 342 metres from the ground, offers a perspective that is only enjoyed by the very brave.

The original and popular 360 revolving restaurant, which of course provides a constantly changing view, was recently renovated and now features the world's tallest wine cellar. The cellar, opened in May 1997, is located in the centre of the restaurant. It resembles a classic underground European-style wine cellar with climate and humidity controls and a 9,000-bottle storage capacity.

The most recent changes result from a $26 million revitalization and expansion in 1998. Interactive multi-media displays, state-of-the-art computer simulations, the Marketplace Café and Edge Arcade are some of the many new hot spots.

Aside from its many features and world records, the CN Tower serves as a compass point for all those in and approaching Toronto. It is a magnificent and familiar southern point and one that is internationally recognized as the world-class structure that it is.

The glass floor, 342 metres above ground level, offers a thrilling view.

The CN Tower reaches 553 metres into the sky.

For any tourist who finds the CN Tower, it's hard to miss the domed structure beside it. The **SkyDome** is by far the world's most modern and luxurious ballpark. Completed in 1989, this renowned facility is home to the world-champion Toronto Blue Jays Baseball Club and to the Toronto Argonauts Football Club. This is a well-loved venue for many reasons, but it is best known for its retractable roof.

When the weather is agreeable, usually from early spring to mid-fall, the roof rolls back to uncover the complete field area and more than 91 per cent of the spectator seats. This roof, which earned the venue its nickname 'the Dome,' has four parts equalling a total width of 209 metres. One part is stationary, while the remaining three move, folding in to reveal the blue sky, sunshine and an abstract view of the CN Tower – and all within 20 minutes.

The roof is not the only feature breaking records at the SkyDome. The $17-million Jumbo Tron is one of the largest video display boards in the world. At a height of three storeys and a width of nine, this super TV gives everyone an amazing view of what's going on. A full production control facility, with five-camera input and a crew of 26, projects the jumbo-size images and information.

Aside from these modern features, the SkyDome is impressive for its size alone. If needed, the field alone could hold 743 Indian elephants or eight Boeing 747s, and how about a 31-storey building? And that's with the roof closed. The structure is large enough to hold the Eaton Centre or the Roman Coliseum. This size is perfect for the sports events that take place here, as well as concerts, trade shows and special events. Believe it or not, the Dome can be an intimate place as well. The SkyTent Arena is an acoustic system that encloses one section of the SkyDome. This allows for a seating capacity from 10,000 to 30,000 – perfect for performances such as Walt Disney's World on Ice, the Harlem Globetrotters and the Garden Bros. Circus.

Some visitors love the SkyDome so much they never want to leave, and they don't have to, since the 348-room SkyDome Hotel is right on site. This four-star accommodation is unique to say the least, with rooms that overlook the field or the city, and all the trimmings including top-notch fitness facilities, restaurants, a Kids' Room and more. The best way to see all the SkyDome has to offer is to take advantage of the highly recommended behind-the-scenes walking tour.

The versatility of a retractable roof makes the SkyDome a popular venue.

World Waterpark is the world's largest indoor waterpark.

The Mindbender Rollercoaster features consecutive double loops and spiralling twists.

Nowhere else in the world would someone dream of spending more than a day at a shopping mall. But at the world's largest shopping complex, located in Edmonton, Alberta, there's a lot more to do than shop. The **West Edmonton Mall** features more than 800 shops and services, eight major department stores, more than 100 eateries featuring every food type and atmosphere imaginable, cafés and pubs on 'Bourbon Street,' and a dizzying line up of attractions.

Approximately 140,000 customers per day, almost half of those from the United States, flock to the West Edmonton Mall, where the theme parks and attractions are simply mind boggling. Features include a giant wave pool, a 14-storey roller coaster, an ice rink, a golf course, dozens of movie theatres, bingo, water slides, a casino, submarines and a live dolphin show. Galaxyland Amusement Park and Galaxykids Playpark are very popular spots, as is the World Waterpark, which is the size of five professional football fields. The mall's Marine Life Department is home to over 200 species of animals, including penguins and exotic birds. The Deep Sea Adventure takes passengers to the depths of the 'oceans' in one of four real submarines for a glimpse of lost treasures, coral reefs and rare species of fish. All in all there are hundreds of reasons to forget your shopping list.

The Ice Palace features a National Hockey League-sized ice rink.

Cosmo welcomes children to an out-of-this-world experience at Galaxy Kids Playpark.

After a fun-filled day, the West Edmonton Mall provides a fun way to spend the night – in the Fantasyland Hotel. This hotel contains, among the 355 guest rooms, 127 themed rooms, each promising to fulfill your quest for the ultimate travel adventure. The world's largest shopping mall also boasts 58 mall entrances, more than 15,000 employees and a parking lot made to hold 20,000 vehicles. Shop 'til you drop takes on an entirely new meaning at the West Edmonton Mall.

The Dolphin Lagoon is home to Atlantic bottlenose dolphins.

Canada's east coast is the site of a small and unassuming fishing village that has gained worldwide attention through its simplicity and beauty. It's a wonder the world would notice a village of mostly fishermen, with a total population of just 60 residents. But **Peggy's Cove**, Nova Scotia, about 45 kilometres west of Halifax, is one of the most photographed locations in Canada. It is a picturesque village surrounding a narrow ocean inlet, complete with a lighthouse that stands on the large, smooth granite rocks. Quaint, colourful homes on rugged land, with lobster traps, fish nets and bobbing boats at the spindle-legged dock, evoke sentimental feelings for this special place that stands still in time.

It is time itself that has made this place what it is. The village dates from 1811, but over 10,000 years ago, the last glaciers left huge boulders in this area. Today, it seems that the giants were placed here on purpose, adding character to an already picturesque locale. Earlier on, glaciers had already removed most of the soil and loose rock from the coast, leaving the four and a half million-year-old Devonian granite seen today.

The main focus of this site is the charming lighthouse that sits upon the wave-washed rock beside the sparkling Atlantic waters. Aside from being a nice touch and former operating beacon, the lighthouse is a working summertime post office – the only one in the country run from a lighthouse. It even has its own stamp cancellation, with an image of the lighthouse on it. That's why many visitors opt to send themselves postcards from here.

Another attraction at Peggy's Cove is the stone sculpture by former resident and artist William deGarthe. Born in Finland, this artist came to Canada in 1926 and lived in Peggy's Cove until he died in 1983. His colossal work can be seen carved into the 30.4-metre rock face behind his residence. The 10-year project is a lasting monument to Canadians, depicting 32 fishermen and their families, some of whom still reside in the town.

To ensure that Peggy's Cove remains as it appears today – the typical fishing village that warms the hearts of the world's people – the province of Nova Scotia has designated it as a preservation area.

This stone sculpture depicts Peggy Cove's fishermen and their families.

◀ *The charming lighthouse at Peggy's Cove adds to
an already picturesque Canadian scene.*

When travelling to Vancouver Island, British Columbia, from the east, signs for this attraction begin as early on as Banff, Alberta. **Butchart Gardens** have been rated among the most beautiful gardens in the world. Nearly one million people from around the world visit this site each year to enjoy the exquisite beauty, floral variety and entertainment. It is ironic that this beautiful expanse was once an empty quarry site.

Robert Pim Butchart made his fortune from Portland cement at the turn of the century in his native Ontario. He was enticed by the rich limestone deposits, important in the making of cement, on the west coast of the country. So he moved his family to Tod Inlet on Vancouver Island in 1904 to build a new factory. As he exhausted the limestone quarry near their new home, his wife decided to refurbish the dismal pit that was left behind. She arranged for soil to be brought in by horse and cart to fill the quarry until eventually she had a blooming, spectacular sunken garden.

Jenny Butchart never looked back and by the 1920s word of her gardens had grown to the point where 50,000 people visited annually to see her creation. Today, still under Butchart ownership, there are over one million plants in 700 varieties planted throughout the estate to ensure continuous blooms from March through October. Highlights include favourites like the original Sunken Garden along with the Rose Garden, which replaced the family's 1929 vegetable patch. The symmetrical Italian Garden is where the Butcharts' tennis court used to be and a Japanese Garden, on the sea side of their home, is complete with a couple of cranes to bring visitors good luck.

In all, there are hundreds of species of trees, flowers and bushes. While the daytime is for detail, an evening tour is also a good idea, since concealed and indirect lighting illuminates the gardens casting a fairyland glow on the scene. The magnificent Ross Fountain is also a popular spot by day or night. Saturday evenings during the summer months mean fireworks presentations choreographed to music with the beautiful gardens as a back drop.

The world's obsession with a small farmhouse on Prince Edward Island began with a 1908 novel written by Canadian Lucy Maud Montgomery. The novel, which tells of the tribulations of a fictional red-headed orphan, touched the hearts of so many people that the real-life setting of the book has become a world-renowned attraction.

Montgomery's book, *Anne of Green Gables*, was eventually translated into 20 languages. People travel from all over the world to witness the site that inspired the famous tale of beloved Anne. As many as 10,000 of the island's annual visitors are now from Japan; it is one of the country's top destinations for Japanese travellers because of **Green Gables**. Fortunately, the trip is well worth it. Green Gables, located in Cavendish, has all of the charm and character that Montgomery's book promises. Touring through the delightful farmhouse is like visiting a place from your childhood in which a dear friend once lived. There is no need for a tour guide to explain which room is which – there's Matthew's room, the pantry and of course

Anne's room, where readers learned so much about the heavy-hearted girl. It's laid out attractively, comfortably, and as expected. The period furniture and decor would please even those who are not familiar with the novel.

Outside, the excitement and experience continues with a stroll through Lover's Lane, which sings with idealistic childhood ambiance. The Haunted Woods are no disappointment either; here one identifies with Anne's panic and apprehension over the horrifying possibilities and eerie atmosphere. The trees through here appear ready to grab little girls with wild imaginations.

Aside from the house and surrounding gardens and paths, there is a gift shop on the grounds. There are also several museums and exhibits throughout the island that invite the public to learn about and recognize Lucy Maud Montgomery's role as an author of national and historical significance. Following a path that leads from Green Gables toward the church will bring visitors to the cemetery in which Montgomery is buried.

In less than the short distance of a kilometre, the flat Canadian prairies give way to the immense and awe-inspiring **Canadian Rockies**. These breathtaking beauties reach high into the sky and straddle the Alberta-British Columbia border. It is not hard to believe that it took millions of years for these colossal giants to become what they are today, and still erosion and change continue.

The Rockies are so many things to so many people that it's virtually impossible to capture them completely and from all perspectives. To many they are an opportunity to ski, climb, hike, kayak, resort or camp. To others they are geological wonders. To still others the Rockies are to be appreciated for their flora and fauna. It would take many a vacation to thoroughly see and experience the Canadian Rockies, but one glimpse of them explains why they are such a source of national pride and beauty for Canada.

Much of the Rockies are protected within two of the country's many national parks – Banff and Jasper. These two parks are internationally famous and are the best known of Canada's Heritage Sites. Public access to this area, when the railway reached it in 1883, moved the government to declare it a national park, Canada's first, for reasons of preservation. The world-renowned Banff Springs Hotel, built in the 1880s, was named for the natural hot springs found by two railway workers. Set in the Bow River Valley, the turreted edifice adds a fairytale quality to the already picturesque scene. Banff National Park boasts 25 mountains of 3,000 metres or more in height. It is famous for its skiing and climbing opportunities.

Yoho and Kootenay national parks, in British Columbia, adjoin Banff National Park. The Trans-Canada Highway passes right through this enchanting part of the country; Roger's Pass is one of the most famous railway passes in North America. Takakkaw Falls, the third-highest falls in North America, are found in Yoho. Emerald Lake, perfectly still and green, reflects the beauty of Yoho in its waters. South of Banff is what's known as Kananaskis Country, an outdoor recreational area. The region covers 4,000 square kilometres and offers the best facilities for every outdoor activity from picnicking to skiing. Some events of the 1988 Olympic Winter Games were held at Nakiska in this area.

Lake Louise, northwest of Banff, is known as the jewel of the Rockies. This famous lake sits in a small glacial valley surrounded by snow-capped mountains. Often a perfect reflection in the lake mirrors the magnificent turn-of-the-century Chateau Lake Louise. This magical lake is also famous for its changing colour. The glacial sediment and changing light cause it to turn alternately blue-green, emerald and aqua in colour. The skiing at Lake Louise is arguably the most scenic in Canada. The 230-kilometre Icefields Parkway is one of the most spectacular stretches of highway in the country. Linking Lake Louise with Jasper, it follows a lake-lined valley that makes up the Continental Divide. The mountains through here are the highest and most rugged in the country,

making the many lookout points great opportunities for memorable views. Along the way are the Columbia Icefields, with approximately 30 glaciers. Up to 350 metres thick, these sheets of ice are remnants of the last Ice Age.

Jasper National Park is a wilder, larger and less explored area than Banff. Maligne Lake can be found here. It is the largest of all the glacier-fed lakes and is considered by many people to be the most beautiful. Many choose to cruise around its Spirit Island. Outside of Jasper National Park is Mount Robson Provincial Park. This park showcases the highest Canadian Rockies peak at 3,954 metres. This mountain has been the object of many challenges and expeditions, beginning with the first climb in 1913.

In all, the Rockies make up the largest mountain parkland in the world. The many parks, peaks and valleys hold numerous favourite and special places. Hillsides are blanketed with mountain flowers and an abundance of animals in all shapes and sizes call these parts their home. The Rocky Mountain goat is exclusive to these mountains. With rushing rivers, sparkling glaciers, lush green valleys, snocapped mountains and multicoloured lakes, there is more here than the mind can imagine. These natural wonders provide a true life experience. Spectacularly beautiful and with quite possibly the best scenery in the world, the Canadian Rockies are spiritual, diverse, breathtaking and larger than life.

CANADIANS SHARE THEIR VAST LAND WITH MUCH THAT is wild and natural – or quite possibly, it's the wild that shares with Canadians. After all, only 10 per cent of the country is inhabited by people, whereas most certainly all of Canada features wildlife and natural beauty.

While there are many wild and unique animals in the country, the beaver has long been associated with Canada. The beloved beaver's rise to fame started, ironically, with the fur hat fashion fad. During the peak of the fur trade, 100,000 beaver pelts made their way to Europe each year. As a result the Canadian beaver was close to extinction in the mid-19th century. Luckily, silk hats became the rage and the beaver lived to become an official emblem of Canada in 1975. The fur trade was a huge success and the beaver pelts proved so lucrative that the Hudson's Bay Company honoured the beaver by putting it on the shield of the company's coat of arms in 1678. This was the first of many appearances by the beaver, including one on the first Canadian postage stamp in 1851, which was also the first stamp in the world to depict an animal.

The largest, and possibly the most dangerous, of Canadian animals is the bear. The grizzly, the most notorious type of bear, roams the higher slopes of the western and northern mountains. It can be recognized by its brown fur with whitish tips and a hump behind its neck. The brown bear, which is actually black in colour, can also be seen in the western and northern parts of the country. It's the black bear that is the most common, found across the country, even in populated areas such as campgrounds and cottage areas. The polar bear is a much-loved creature. It can weigh up to 680 kilograms and has thick, off-white fur. This animal is protected by law and can be found only in the extreme north, including many near Churchill, Manitoba, and in zoos.

Other well-known Canadian animals include the buffalo, wolf, coyote, deer, moose, caribou, elk and porcupine. The raccoon and skunk are scavengers that can be found even in big cities in Canada. Raccoons can open even the most securely fitting garbage-can lid; skunks are known for their foul-smelling spray, which they use as a defense mechanism. The Rocky Mountain goat and the lynx, a large gray cat found in remote woodlands, are two animals that are unique to Canada. Whale

The colossal moose is the undisputed king of the antler world.

Its jaunty crest, black necklace and beautiful blue colour identify the blue jay.

The beaver is a much-loved Canadian emblem.

watching in the Pacific and Atlantic waters and on the St. Lawrence River is so popular that it has become a successful commercial enterprise.

There have been more than 500 species of birds spotted in Canada. The loon, a beautiful water bird with a haunting call, is very popular and found most abundantly in northern Ontario. The loon can also be found on the 'loonie' – Canada's one-dollar coin. The great blue heron, one of the country's largest birds is a wonder to see take off. And the Canada goose – a graceful glider – is the most familiar and common of all geese in the country.

Mountains and rugged terrain are common in Canada.

There are many beautiful surprises hidden in Canada's numerous parks.

The majestic great blue heron.

Canada's parks offer much beauty and serenity.

Canada's parks are perfect spots to experience the wild and natural. There are 37 national parks, which serve to protect and preserve. Managed by the federal government, these parks also feature 129 National Historical Sites, which include forts, battle sites, pioneer homesteads and the like.

The Rocky Mountain parks are by far the most popular of the group. In addition to all the beauty and recreation that surrounds the mountains, it is here visitors find the westernmost Canadian Heritage Site – the former Haida Indian Village of Ninstints. This site is believed to have been inhabited by Natives for more than 2,000 years. Experiencing the western edge of the continent is best from Pacific Rim National Park on Vancouver Island. Aside from the amazing surf and sun, the area boasts the oldest

The Cabot Trail, in Cape Breton Highlands National Park, is world-renowned.

and tallest trees in the country. On the other side of the country, Cape Breton Highlands National Park is one of the most scenic places in Canada. It gained its reputation from one of the best-known roads in the country – the Cabot Trail. The road winds right along the shoreline and at times runs up and down steep mountains, past barren plains and through lush valleys. Cyclists and sports car drivers are in heaven here.

Wood Buffalo National Park, on the border of Alberta and the Northwest Territories, is one of the world's largest parks – larger than Switzerland, in fact. This is also the home of the world's largest herd of free-roaming buffalo – 6,000 at last count. It's also the world's only nesting site for the endangered whooping crane. Even further north is Auyuittuq National Park, the only park in the world that is inside the Arctic Circle. Dog sledding, whale watching and genuine Inuit carvings are just a few highlights available on an adventure in this area.

The country also has a huge system of provincial parks run by each individual province. One of Canada's best known is Algonquin Provincial Park, which is Ontario's largest and oldest park, located about 300 kilometres north of Toronto. It is considered a semi-wilderness park and features hundreds of lakes, canoe routes, campgrounds and unpredictable weather and wildlife. The wild and natural aspects of Canada play an important role in the daily lives of the people who live here. It's reflected in the beliefs, arts and culture throughout the country.

THE CANADIAN PEOPLE HAVE MANY FACES, FACES THAT are as diverse and varied as the country's land. Even before Canada grew to include the colourful and distinctive population it does, it was unusual in the fact that it is an officially bilingual nation. The French colonists were the first to carry the name 'Canadians.' Today, Montreal is the second-largest French-speaking city in the world after Paris; there are large concentrations of French-speaking Canadians throughout the entire country. Acadian residents in the bilingual province of New Brunswick speak the French language of the first Atlantic Canada settlers.

Canada is also proud of its multiculturalism. After all, the Native cultures are the only truly indigenous cultures of Canada. However, less than one million people identify themselves exclusively as members of the North American Indian, Inuit or Métis Aboriginal groups. Ontario has the highest concentration of Aboriginal people, but the Northwest Territories has the highest proportion, with 60 per cent of its population being of Aboriginal descent. All other Canadians immigrated from elsewhere, whether it was hundreds of years ago or just recently.

Much of the Canadian population is made up of British descendants. Almost four million Canadians are of Scottish or Irish ancestry. Other major groups are German, Italian, Ukrainian, Dutch, Greek, Polish, Portuguese, Scandinavian – literally every nationality imaginable. More recently, Asians, especially Chinese immigrating from Hong Kong, Latin Americans and people from the Caribbean have been immigrating in larger numbers. Canada also receives refugees from all over the world.

Most newcomers head to the larger cities. Toronto, as a result, is one of the most cosmopolitan cities in the world.

In 1988, the multicultural character of the country was officially recognized when the Government of Canada passed the Multiculturalism Act. This act is for the preservation and enhancement of multiculturalism in Canada. Canadians have embraced this idea of preservation, allowing each separate culture to flourish. Many cultures have their own neighbourhoods and newspapers as well as radio and television stations. Canadians love the opportunities that lie in its Chinatowns, Little Italies, and Greek Towns, and in the many restaurants, delicatessens and bakeries found there. A walk through Toronto's Kensington Market provides a small but accurate sampling of the wide variety of culture and cuisine Canadians have to offer and enjoy.

How can 30 million people from all ends of the earth live happily in one nation? Through a mixture of different cultures, races, religions and languages, Canadians have unity in diversity. Their strong sense of national identity comes through the mature acceptance, open recognition and celebration of a diverse cultural heritage.

Generally, Canadians are polite and friendly people. They are welcomed around the world as tourists and kidded about their use of the word 'eh.' It is thought that their 'eh?' at the end of a statement (most typically imitated as "How's it going eh?") is an invitation for people to respond and to agree. Canadians love to get along, and perhaps that's why they do.

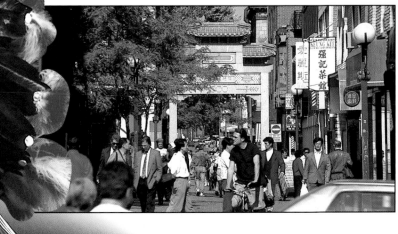

CANADIANS LOVE A CELEBRATION AND FIND REASONS to celebrate, congregate and socialize all year round. On the first day of each year Canadians across the country participate in what's known as the New Year's Day Polar Bear Swim. This event involves a quick dip in the ocean or lake – quick because January is the coldest month of the year in all provinces of the country.

Chinese New Year is also celebrated across the country, and not just by Chinese Canadians. Vancouver's Chinatown is known for hosting the loudest and most colourful of celebrations. Also on the west coast is the International Dragon Boat Festival in June. This three-day event draws some 2,000 competitors and 150,000 spectators. The Abbotsford International Air Show, which takes place each year in August just outside of Vancouver, has been voted the worlds' best and features everything from gliders to the Concorde.

The Calgary Stampede is an event to top all events. This 10-day festival, dating from 1912, is known worldwide. The rodeo, which is the highlight of the activities, is the biggest and toughest in North America. A parade, nighttime shows, amusement rides and lots of cowboys and bucking broncos are served up at this western Canadian festival.

Up in the Northwest Territories, each March brings with it excitement around the Caribou Carnival. Aside from the entertainment, parade and igloo-building contests, the Canadian Championship Dog Derby takes place. This three-day race is approximately 240 kilometres long. The Winnipeg Folk Festival, held annually for three days in the summer, is the country's biggest and best known. It features more than 200 concerts, crafts and international cuisine.

The International Dragon Boat Festival, British Columbia.

Winterlude turns winter into magic each February in Ottawa.

The rodeo is the highlight of the Calgary Stampede.

The Canadian National Exhibition takes place in Toronto each summer.

Powwows are frequent events all across Canada.

Toronto is a hot spot for festivals and events. There's something for everyone here, especially during the summer months, including the Toronto International Powwow held at SkyDome, the Gay Pride Day Parade, which passes through the gay and lesbian district of the city's downtown, and Caribana, an annual West Indian festival. Caribana has attracted over a million people to marvel at the costumes and party along with the reggae and calypso-beat parade, which has been known to last a full 10 hours. The annual Molson Indy race is on the international circuit and takes place along Toronto's Lakeshore Boulevard. From cars to horses, Toronto is also host to the annual Queen's Plate held at Woodbine Race Track – one of North America's oldest horse races. This city is also home to the Canadian National Exhibition – the world's largest and the oldest of its kind. It includes a midway of rides; agricultural, technical and multicultural displays and events; concerts; crafts; an air show and just about everything in between, including fireworks.

The annual Royal St. John's Regatta takes place on Quidi Vidi Lake in Newfoundland.

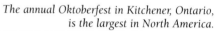

The annual Oktoberfest in Kitchener, Ontario, is the largest in North America.

The Stratford Shakespearean Festival is well respected.

The internationally recognized Queen's Plate horse race takes place at Woodbine Race Track in Toronto, Ontario.

The Shaw Festival, held from April to October each year in Niagara-on-the-Lake, Ontario, is the only festival in the world dedicated to the plays of George Bernard Shaw and his contemporaries. In Stratford, Ontario, many respected actors have graced the stages of the Stratford Shakespearean Festival. Beginning in a tent in 1953, today it is an internationally recognized event featuring the best of everything. For those interested in a festival that involves more beer than poetry, the world-renowned Oktoberfest in Kitchener, Ontario, features 20 beer halls. With beer steins, bratwurst and laderhosen galore, this event is the largest of its kind in North America, with 500,000 people attending annually.

The cold and snow do not knock the festival mood out of Canadians. The Winter Carnival in Quebec City is a famous annual event that takes place during the deep freeze of February. Ice sculptures, snow games, a parade and the lovable Bonhomme, the large French snowman who serves as carnival mascot and symbol, draw everyone outdoors and from afar. While people on the east coast enjoy parties year round, the annual Highland Games, held in Antigonish, Nova Scotia, each year in July, is a major event. Pipe bands, dancers and athletes have been entertaining and participating since 1861. Over on the island of Newfoundland, the annual Royal St. John's Regatta closes down the town on the first Wednesday of August. This rowing competition, held at the shores of Quidi Vidi Lake, began in 1826 and is the oldest continuous sporting event in North America.

There are countless festivals and events of numerous types happening across the country of Canada each year. It is a nation that enjoys a party and has much to celebrate – a wonderful combination.

Highland Games, Antigonish, Nova Scotia.

Caribana is an annual West Indian festival that includes a very popular parade.

The Winter Carnival in Quebec City is world-renowned.

IN THE MATTER OF ARTS, CANADIANS ARE DESERVING OF credit and recognition in many fields. Many artists, be they singers, musicians, actors or painters, are worthy of international attention but often remain little known unless they leave their home country. Still others are just plain famous, and seem always to have been.

Canadian painters have become known for their works depicting nature – most often Canadian scenery. The best-known remain the Group of Seven. They dominated Canadian art for three decades and remain popular both at home and internationally. Their inspiration was drawn from the Canadian geography in the eastern lakelands area. Emily Carr painted western Canada in a similar fashion but, of course, with Native accents such as totem poles. Today, Robert Bateman is widely known for his take on nature and his work is surprisingly affordable. The best place to see Canadian art is at the McMichael Canadian Collection in Kleinburg, Ontario. This gallery is the only major public gallery that is completely dedicated to Canadian art. It is known as the home of many works by Canada's famous Group of Seven and also displays a spectacular collection of work by First Nations and Inuit artists. Native Indians are well known and admired for their sculptures, carvings, prints, jewellery and bead work.

There has been an impressive amount of quality writing produced in this country. Poets such as EJ Pratt, Irving Layton and Leonard Cohen are among many who have made their mark. Novelists and short-story writers have done very well internationally. Best known names include Margaret Atwood, Robertson Davies, Margaret Laurence, Alice Munro and Mordecai Richler. Most good bookstores will have a Canadian section these days, and with good reason.

Emily Carr 1871-1945, Corner of Kitwancool Village, c. 1930, oil on canvas, 111.5 x 68.0 cm, McMichael Canadian Art Collection. Gift of Dr. and Mrs. Max Stern, Dominion Gallery, Montreal, 1977.42.

Canadian art is not limited to indoor galleries. Street artists add to the charm of many cities, as shown here in Quebec City (left) and Old Montreal.

Inuit soapstone carver
in Pangnirtung,
Nunavut.

Chemainus, British Columbia, is famous for its larger-than-life murals.

Lawren S. Harris 1885-1970, Snow c. 1917, oil on canvas, 71.0 x 110.1 cm, gift of Mr. and Mrs. Keith MacIver,
McMichael Canadian Art Collection, 1966.16.88.

There's too much going on in Canadian music to cover it adequately. Canada's singers and musicians cross many categories and all boundaries. Among the best known internationally are pianist Glenn Gould, guitarist Liona Boyd, composer R. Murray Schafer and jazz musician Oscar Peterson. Naturally, folk and country music has been appreciated in Canada with names like Gordon Lightfoot, Joni Mitchell, Stompin' Tom, Neil Young, kd lang and Shania Twain. Anne Murray, The Rankin Family, Ashley MacIsaac and the Irish Descendants have made Canada proud with their unique east coast talents. Traditional Canadian singers in the Native category include big names like Buffy Sainte Marie and Susan Aglukark.

Of course, Canadians know how to rock too. Kim Mitchell, Jeff Healy, Brian Adams, Celine Dion and Sarah McLaughlan are among many who have gone far. And Canada is not without its collection of instrumentalists. The Montreal Symphony Orchestra, one of many, has a well-established reputation for its diversity and versatility. As well, there are a huge number of exciting and talented singers, musicians and bands who have 'made it' but remain for Canadian ears only.

They're not often Hollywood blockbusters, and are not meant to be, but Canadian films have gained tremendous respect worldwide. The National Film Board of Canada, created in 1939, is a public agency that produces

The former home of world-renowned author Margaret Laurence has been preserved as a municipal heritage site in Manitoba.

Canadian singer Anne Murray has recorded more than 30 albums.

The National Film Board movie Momentum, features many Canadian events such as figure skating, in which Canadians excel.

The International Jazz Festival, held annually in Montreal, is a popular summer event featuring world-famous jazz musicians.

and distributes films that reflect Canada and its citizens, and the rest of the world. Annual releases include a variety of animation, documentary and drama. In addition to supporting its own commercial film industry, Canada has become a prime location for shooting international films because of its diverse scenery and highly skilled visual and audio professionals – all at a cheaper price than in many other parts of the world. The Montreal World Film Festival, the largest publicly attended film festival in the western world, ranks among such prestigious festivals as those in Cannes, Berlin and Venice.

From the screen to the stage, Canada's largest city, Toronto, is recognized as the world's third-largest theatre centre after New York and London. There are over 200 professional theatre and dance companies here, including venues that support Broadway shows and musicals. The Pantages Theatre on Yonge Street has an indefinite run of Andrew Lloyd Webber's *Phantom of the Opera* on stage. Many big-name hits come and go in venues such as the Royal Alexandra Theatre, Princess of Wales Theatre and Elgin Theatre, to name a few. The Stratford Festival, located in Stratford, Ontario, attracts and trains the world's best actors. This not-for-profit repertory theatre festival produces the best in classical and contemporary theatre with a special emphasis on the works of Shakespeare. Also on stage in Toronto is the National Ballet of Canada. With more than 60 dancers and a full symphony orchestra, it ranks as one of the world's top international dance companies. Founded in 1959, Canada's National Ballet School is one of the world's finest for professionals who go on to perform not only classics, but also contemporary works developed in Canada.

CANADIANS LOVE THEIR SPORTS. THEY WATCH THEM, they play them and they talk about them. Even though Canada's official national sport is lacrosse, a Native Indian game played with nets on sticks and a small ball, it's hockey that Canadians are most passionate about. The game of hockey was invented in Canada and is definitely the country's most important contribution to the world of sports. The first game was played in Montreal in 1879 by McGill University students. Today it is played professionally in over 20 countries.

There are a number of local, provincial and national amateur hockey teams across the country. It's also quite common for people to play what are referred to as 'pick-up' games just for fun. The wooden side boards of outdoor rinks smack with slap shots for most of the winter months. And winter weekends for many families across the country mean five or six a.m. time slots for children's hockey teams at local arenas. It's more than a pastime, it's a way of life. Children dream of being on a Stanley Cup-winning National Hockey League (NHL) team some day.

The Montreal Canadiens is a favourite team in the National Hockey League.

The Hockey Hall of Fame is home to many hockey treasures including the original Stanley Cup.

Blue Jays pitcher sports a special uniform worn when playing a game on Canada Day.

National Basketball Association members the Vancouver Grizzlies draw huge crowds of fans.

The Stanley Cup was donated by Canadian Governor General Frederick Arthur, Lord Stanley of Preston, in 1892 to be given annually to the best Canadian hockey team. Today both American and Canadian hockey teams, members of the NHL, which was formed in 1917, compete each season for the Stanley Cup trophy.

Hockey stars are more than famous athletes, they are Canadian legends. Names like the legendary Maurice 'Rocket' Richard and the 'Great' Wayne Gretzky have become a part of Canadian history, as have the words 'Hockey Night in Canada.' It was hockey announcer Foster Hewitt's play-by-play for *Hockey Night in Canada*, over the radio airwaves and later on television, that helped secure hockey as a national game. There are six NHL teams in Canada: the Montreal Canadiens, Toronto Maple Leafs,

Ottawa Senators, Calgary Flames, Edmonton Oilers and Vancouver Canucks.

Other professional sports organizations in Canada include the Canadian Football League (CFL), which plays a faster and more challenging game than the American league, but is less popular with football fans. Still, the championship game known as the Grey Cup is a recognized national event. Baseball is very popular in Canada at many levels. The two teams in the major leagues are the Montreal Expos and the Toronto Blue Jays. Canada recently joined the American professional basketball league with the Vancouver Grizzlies and the Toronto Raptors. Both teams have increased the popularity of the National Basketball Association (NBA) and team shirts from all teams can be seen worn throughout the country.

Canada offers world-class skiing opportunities.

Mountain biking is a favourite pastime all across Canada.

Lacrosse is Canada's national sport.

*Watersports are popular
from coast to coast.*

Canadians themselves participate in every sport imaginable. With their multicultural diversity, variety of climates and disparate geography, everything is possible in both organized and individual sport. Cycling, sailing, ice-fishing, skating, hiking, mountain climbing, archery, fishing, hunting, running, canoeing … the list is seemingly endless. One sport that Canada is distinctly known and appreciated for, however, is skiing. There are four main alpine ski centres in the country – Ontario, Quebec, Alberta and British Columbia.

Golfing in Whistler, British Columbia.

Ontario's skiing takes place a two-to three-hour drive north of Toronto. The most challenging is at Collingwood's Blue Mountain. There are about 20 ski centres within two hours of Montreal. The snow, scenery and hills here are fabulous thanks to the slopes of the Laurentian Mountains; with Mont Tremblant offering the longest vertical drop. There is also skiing in the Appalachian Mountains. The skiing around Quebec City is premier as well, with Mont Sainte-Anne being the most popular destination. It also offers some of the best cross-country ski trails. But it's the skiing in the west that puts Canada on the map with international downhill lovers. Alberta's Rocky Mountains rate international status. The giant hills at Banff and Lake Louise offer runs higher than any in the European Alps. British Columbia's Whistler Resort is a major stop for tourists and hosts many international competitions.

All in all, the sporting opportunities in Canada are unlimited.

Banking, insurance, education and other service industries are a large part of the Canadian economy.

Red-hot slag pouring.

48

M UCH OF CANADA'S ECONOMY IS DERIVED FROM the country's abundant natural resources. The country's most valuable and renewable resource are its forests. Pulp, paper, lumber and other wood products are made from the timber of a productive forest. Canada's forests are so productive, in fact, that Canada is the world's largest exporter of forest products. This results in the vital need for management to protect mature forests and new growth against misuse, fire, insects and disease. The Canadian Forest Service is dedicated to promoting sustainable development of the forests while allowing the forestry industry to remain competitive for present and future Canadians.

Canada also has one of the largest commercial fishing industries in the world. One of the richest fishing grounds in the world is off the coast of Newfoundland. The Grand Banks are a shallow continental shelf that extends about 400 kilometres. The mixing of ocean currents at this location has provided a favourable climate for an abundance of fish. This is, however, a vulnerable resource and one that must be managed wisely.

Minerals, natural gas, oil and hydroelectricity are also major elements in the Canadian economy. Alberta has the largest deposits of oil and natural gas in Canada and most of the country's known coal deposits are here. Mining is a way of life for Canadians across the country for every-

Saskatchewan grows most of the country's wheat.

thing from nickel, zinc and copper to gold, aluminum and iron. Water power has been the traditional source of electrical energy in the country. Manufacturing, mostly of vehicles and in high technology such as space and computers, is also a factor in the economy. For example, the Canadarm was manufactured for the US space shuttle program. But surprisingly, the largest part of the economy in Canada is the service industry. A large civil service sector, as well as banking, communication, insurance and education, bring in much of the country's foreign exchange.

Aside from its abundant forests, Canada is probably best known for its agricultural attributes. While only a small percentage of this vast country is suitable for agriculture, because of the harsh climate, this industry is very successful. A major portion of Canadian crops are used for making cereal grains, forage crops and oil seeds such as canola and flax, soybean and sunflower. Most appreciated is Canada's wheat. The fields of this popular grain are quite a sight, especially during harvesting season when huge self-powered combine harvesters thresh their way through seas of the golden crop. The first cultivated wheat in the world was grown on the south shore of the North Saskatchewan River in 1754.

There has been many a successful Canadian farmer, but one in particular, Herman Trelle of Grande Prairie, Alberta, may have been the best in the world. Between 1926 and 1934 he won 135 international awards for his flax, rye, oats and wheat. In fact, he won the world's wheat growing championship at the Chicago International Grain Show so many times that he was barred from entering for four years to give other farmers a chance to win. Today, Saskatchewan is the major wheat growing province, and the hard spring wheat grown on the prairies is world-renowned for its quality. Wheat and barley account for most of Canada's agricultural exports.

Canada is also known for its fruit during the summer season. Lakes Erie and Ontario contribute to an extended number of frost-free days for the cultivation of peaches, pears and other fruit, including grapes. Canadian grapevines are of high enough quality to have gained the country a name for its wines in the past decade. The Niagara Peninsula in Ontario and British Columbia's Okanagan Valley are the two main wine-producing regions in the country. The dry white wines are very popular and the ice wines have been declared by critics to be among the best in the world. The ice wines produced in Ontario must be made within stricter laws than those of Germany, where ice wine is thought to have originated.

Canada's most important fruit, in terms of dollars for crops, is the apple. The most distinctive of these is the McIntosh. While clearing a farm in Ontario in 1811, Canadian settler John McIntosh found a small tree that grew a tasty fruit. He started a nursery and developed the now-famous McIntosh apple.

The apple is Canada's most valuable fruit crop.

Canola is a major Canadian crop.

Vineyards are abundant in both Ontario and British Columbia.

Canadian wines have become world-renowned and have won many awards in the past decade.

IN THE WORDS OF THE FIRST PRIME MINISTER OF CANADA, Sir John A. Macdonald, Canada's government is "A general government and legislature for general purposes with local government and legislatures for local purposes." And that's basically how it works – there are federal and provincial governments with various forms of local government.

Canada has a British-style government, in which a parliament consists of the queen, the Senate and the House of Commons. The Queen (of England) is more a symbolic participant as the Queen of Canada and appoints a governor general to act on her behalf in a purely ceremonial manner. A prime minister and his cabinet answer to the 282-member House of Commons. This arrangement comes about through a democratic vote that results in a maximum five-year term. The Senate, mostly retired politicians appointed on the advice of the prime minister, is mainly for consultation. Provincial governments have a fair amount of autonomy, with an elected premier governing areas such as education and natural resources. Because they are not provinces, the Yukon, Nunavut and Northwest territories depend more on Ottawa as the capital of the country and on its federal laws. Aboriginal peoples have long sought independence in the form of self-government and have achieved some of this recently. The balancing of powers between federal, provincial and the northern territories is ongoing.

One political issue that has gained international attention in the past is the province of Quebec and its move toward separation from the rest of Canada. It is an issue that seems never to be resolved or clarified. The idea of leaving Canada first became an organized political movement in the 1960s. French-Canadian radicals used terrorism to gain attention for their cause. The Parti Québécois (PQ) won the provincial election in 1976. Part of its platform was to secure independence for Quebec. The first referendum on the separation issue, in 1980, resulted in a 60 per cent vote to stay. The issue was dropped for a short time. The PQ wanted to try again and held another referendum in 1995. Once again the majority of Quebec voters wanted to stay, but the margin was less than one per cent. In response, the federal government has given up much of its power to the provinces, but still rumours remain of a third referendum and the French desire for a 'distinct society.' What is meant by the term distinct society remains, unfortunately, unclear to the rest of Canada.

The House of Commons is the focal point of parliamentary activity, where national and international issues are debated.

The Canadian flag blows proudly atop the Peace Tower, on the Centre Block of the Parliament Buildings.

This famous address – 24 Sussex Drive – is home to Canada's prime minister.

MADE IN CANADA

CANADA HAS A HISTORY OF BRIGHT IDEAS AND SUCcessful inventions. The world of sports would be a different place without the country's contributions. Not only was hockey invented in Canada, but so was hockey's goalie mask. In 1959 Fibreglass Canada and Montreal Canadiens goalie Jacques Plante developed the first mask after Plante sustained countless injuries to his face. Aside from giving hockey to the world, basketball and five-pin bowling were invented here, as were rollerskates, ski-binding and lacrosse. The snowmobile was invented out of necessity about 50 years ago by J. Armand Bombardier.

From athletics to appetites, the Canadian-born baby food, Pablum was invented at the Hospital for Sick Children in Toronto in the 1920s. Canada

Snowmobiles were first produced at the Bombardier Co. factory.

was also the birthplace of favourites such as ice brewed beer, Smarties and Red Rose Tea. The first chocolate bar was invented and sold in New Brunswick in 1910, by the owner of a small bakery shop, James H. Gagnon. He invented the five-cent chocolate nut bar for his customers to take on fishing trips.

Technology has played a big role in Canadian inventions, starting with Alexander Graham Bell, who invented the telephone here. The country also has provided the AM radio, walkie-talkie, cable television, the IMAX projector and most recently the Canadarm for the space shuttle. The list is endless and includes everything from the push-up bra, zipper, Jolly Jumper, Superman and time zones to the air-conditioned vehicle and Trivial Pursuit.

TRANSPORTATION

THE HISTORY OF CANADIAN TRANSPORTATION IS TIED very closely to the history of the country itself. Successful transportation has been, and continues to be, a triumph over geography and climate. The vast size of the country is an obvious factor, but there are also rugged mountain ranges, dense forests and changing climates to consider year round. Snow and ice must be removed from roads, highways, runways and railway tracks. Many waterways can be used for transportation only during warmer months. However, despite these challenges, Canada has a sophisticated transportation system that involves everything from airplanes, trains and subways to personal cars and snowmobiles.

Aside from shoes, canoes and animals, Canada's transportation began with the Canadian Pacific Railway (CPR). The last spike of North America's first transcontinental railway was driven into mountain rock in British Columbia on November 7, 1885. The project had taken a mere

54 months – six years less than had been predicted. The railway played a large role in the political integration and economic development of Canada, bringing the east and the west together and carrying the first European settlers across the country. Many western cities grew around CPR stations. Today the railways are still one of the main forms of freight transportation – the CPR and the Canadian National Railway operate most national rail freight services. Intercity train companies and VIA Rail run passenger trains. In all, the railway transportation network incorporates approximately 71,000 kilometres of rail lines.

With a coastline as extensive as Canada's, water routes play a dominant role in the country's transportation network. There are hundreds of ports across the country, with most of the deep-water ports located on the east and west coasts and along the St. Lawrence Seaway. The St. Lawrence Seaway is one of the world's longest inland waterways, stretching 3,700 kilometres from the Atlantic to the west-

Canada boasts many means of transportation, from lift locks and icefield vehicles to helicopters and seaplanes.

The passenger and freight train, which began the technology of transportation in Canada, remains a popular means of transport today.

Trilium Terminal 3, from which Canadian Airlines operates, is a modern and architecturally stunning portion of Pearson International Airport in Toronto.

ern end of Lake Superior. Most parts of the seaway are open year round, allowing ocean going vessels to travel deep into the continent – a triumph of engineering. The BC Ferries Corporation is the world's largest ferry system and has made Tsawwassen the most active port in Canada. This system services close to 50 ports of call on 25 routes throughout coastal British Columbia. On the east coast, Marine Atlantic provides a major link between Newfoundland and the rest of the country. Its fleet boasts Canada's two largest superferries.

From sea to sky, Canada is well equipped and connected for air travel. The country's main airports are in Vancouver, Toronto, Montreal and Halifax. Serving both domestic and international routes are Canadian Airlines International and Air Canada, the country's two main carriers. Aside from business and holiday travel, air transportation is very important in many of the country's northern areas, which are inaccessible by any other means,

and rely on bush pilots and larger craft for transportation and supplies. In most other parts of the country roads provide one of the most highly used forms of freight transportation. About half of the total freight revenue goes to the transport trucking industry. Of course, Canada's roads are widely used by personal vehicles for transportation. The automobile is the most popular form of personal transport in the country. There is at least one automobile for every two Canadians. The Trans-Canada Highway, completed in 1962, is the longest national highway in the world at 7,775 kilometres.

Canadians have successfully overcome the obstacles to efficient transportation with intelligent and flexible solutions. They lead the way in transportation technology, in part because of the demanding conditions faced in the past – the same conditions of varied geography and precipitation that will continue to face them in the future.

The Royal Canadian Mounted Police wear official garb for ceremonial events.

✦ ROYAL CANADIAN MOUNTED POLICE

A RED-UNIFORM-CLAD MOUNTIE, STANDING PROUDLY beside a shining horse on the rugged frontier is certainly an image that screams "Canada." The Royal Canadian Mounted Police (RCMP) are indeed a national icon and living symbol of Canadian heritage. But this vital organization is much more complex than the movies of yesterday, and the television shows of today, make it out to be.

The RCMP formed as the North-West Mounted Police (NWMP) in 1873. At the time, Canadians were struggling to settle in the western part of the country. The famous NWMP march west to ease tensions between the settlers and the Natives began the following year. A succession of duties followed, including policing the travelling labour force of the Canadian Pacific Railway, built to join the east with the west. The Klondike Gold Rush and two world wars followed. By the 1920s the renamed RCMP established friendly relations with Native groups, controlled

whiskey traders, supervised treaties between the Indian tribes and the government and generally eased the hardships of the times. The RCMP have been in most chapters and many headlines of Canadian history.

Every detail of the colourful history of the RCMP can be found at the RCMP Centennial Museum and Depot in Regina, Saskatchewan. Uniforms, replicas and stories of some of the famous exploits of the force are on display. The training facilities and barracks also can be toured. In addition to this, a drill takes place at 1 p.m. each weekday.

Today, the RCMP are in the information age and continue to enforce laws made by the authority of the Canadian Parliament. A computerized access system for criminal information has been in operation since 1972. The first female recruits became RCMP members in 1974 and since then, recruiting has also reflected a multicultural Canada. On top of their national security responsibilities, they still police many of the country's western and remote towns.

Mounties are not often seen fighting crime in their red coats and uniform hats; however, certain members of the RCMP can be seen in full and official garb in ceremonial escorts, parades and celebrations in Canada and abroad. A favourite and famous exercise of the Mounties is the RCMP Musical Ride. This combination of history, power, precision and beauty leaves a lasting impression on anyone, but especially a proud Canadian. The Musical Ride was developed out of a desire by the early members to amuse themselves while practising and displaying their riding ability – at the same time they entertained their community. The first known riding display was given in 1876 and the first Musical Ride was performed in 1897 at the Regina barracks.

Until 1966, every member of the RCMP did recruit equitation training, but now only those who have applied and been accepted for Musical Ride duty learn how to ride in this traditional way. The Musical Ride is perfected at the RCMP Stables and Practice Ground in Ottawa. The public is always welcome to watch the practice sessions, but the greatest time to experience it is during the week leading up to Canada Day, when there is a Musical Ride, with full band, each evening in the capital.

The Royal Canadian Mounted Police are a national icon and living symbol of Canadian heritage.

UP IN THE NORTHWEST CORNER OF THE COUNTRY is the great territory of Yukon. It is a rugged place with high plateaus, lowland river valleys and a tundra plain along the Arctic coast. Half of the territory is forested and many mountains feature permanent ice caps. The temperture range is very dramatic, with long cold winters and short, but warm and dry, summers. It is here that the continent's earliest undisputed evidence of human habitation was found. Caves dating back 20,000 years on the Bluefish River revealed stone tools and animal bones. This is a great and ancient place and home to the country's highest point – Mount Logan. The tourism industry is becoming just as important as mining, fishing, forestry and furs.

Mount Logan is the highest point in the country.

The capital city and government centre of Yukon is Whitehorse, located on the banks of the Yukon River, where two thirds of the province's population lives. Yukon Native Indian groups make up a significant portion of this population. The Alaska Highway leads right into the city, where a number of attractions await. Among these is the Old Log Church Museum, which is said to be the only wooden cathedral in the world. It's also the oldest building in Whitehorse, built by the town's first priest in 1900.

Dawson City is another popular spot and one that evokes images of the gold rush. The Dawson City Museum has an amazing collection of 25,000 gold rush artefacts. There is still gold to be found by panning in nearby creeks. For those who want a little entertainment with their riches, Diamond Tooth Gertie's Gambling Hall is a great place to relive the good old days. Gertie's is a fabulous recreation of an 1898 saloon, complete with a honky-tonk piano, dancing girls and gambling a plenty. For a unique experience visitors can take Highway 9 or, as it's most often referred to, the Top of the World Highway, for a scenic drive. The gravel road winds 108 kilometres to the Alaska border.

The main road in this territory is, of course, the Alaska Highway. One of the major engineering feats of the 20th century, the Alaska Highway was built in 1942 as part of the war effort. The highway was built by Canadian and US soldiers and Native Indians, who worked at a pace of 12 kilometres a day in order to beat the approaching winter weather. The highway starts in British Columbia and ends in Alaska – approximately 2,450 kilometres in all. The highway route followed a series of air fields during wartime, but today it is the road to many beautiful sights and cities in one of the country's most interesting areas.

Whitehorse is the government centre of this territory.

The Alaska Highway is the main road in the Yukon Territory.

Beautiful Dawson City sits on the Yukon River amid a nest of mountains.

The magnificent aurora borealis fill the northern skies each winter and early spring.

NORTHWEST TERRITORIES

THE NORTHWEST TERRITORIES, AND THE NEW TERRITORY of Nunavut as of April 1999, cover the top third of the country – all the way to the true North Pole. This is a land of midnight sun and pristine wilderness, office towers and igloos. Nearly half of this region is north of the Arctic Circle. This is truly a place of contrasts with both Arctic and subarctic temperatures, barren tundra and dense forests, and where there are more caribou than people. Among the people are the Native Dene, Inuit and Métis, who collectively speak eight official languages.

Yellowknife, on the northern shores of Great Slave Lake, is the largest town in the Northwest Territories and serves as the government, service and commercial centre for the region. Aside from the enchanting and rocky landscape

and many nearby lakes, there are a number of popular attractions here. The Legislative Assembly, with its domed roof, contains the country's only round legislative chamber (this is probably the only chamber with a polar bear rug in the middle of the floor as well). The design symbolizes the northern people's traditional consensus style of dealing with issues. The Prince of Wales Northern Heritage Centre effectively displays a history of the territories and of aviation in the Northwest Territories. This is also a good place to appreciate Native arts and craft work.

Nahanni National Park, which can be reached only by air, attracts visitors from around the world to experience the magnificent wilderness, which includes the MacKenzie

With its domed roof, the round Legislative Assembly resembles an igloo.

Drying fish.

Nahanni National Park is home to the spectacular and mighty Virginia Waterfalls.

Mountains and many spectacular canyons and waterfalls. It is here that the mighty Virginia Waterfalls drop from twice the height of Niagara Falls. Aside from the many opportunities for hiking, soaking in hot springs and spotting wildlife, the South Nahanni River offers the best whitewater rafting on the continent.

Another excellent feature of these northern territories is the always magical aurora borealis. From about December to April each year, the northern lights, as they're known, dance across the skies. A faint greenish glow, or a golden streak, bring a warm and spiritual quality to the land below. This brilliant sight, which can sometimes be seen from the northern parts of the provinces below, is created by solar winds flowing through the earth's magnetosphere.

NUNAVUT

NUNAVUT TERRITORY, WHICH MEANS 'OUR LAND,' WAS created as a result of a land settlement for an Aboriginal rights agreement between the Inuit and the Canadian government. One of the world's largest islands, Baffin Island, is found in this territory. The Inuit, who have lived here for thousands of years, chose Iqaluit to be their capital. Located on the east coast of Baffin Island, it is one of the largest centres in the territory. Icebergs, wilderness and breathtaking scenery are a part of the Nunavut experience, as is the recognition that the Inuit, now working not only outdoors but in business and government, were still nomadic and living off the land a few short decades ago. Nunavut attractions are truly beautiful and unique as the Inuit are skilled artisans and

Traditional Inuit drums are used for entertainment and for ceremonial or spiritual activities.

Iqaluit is both the seat of government and major transportation centre of Nunavut.

keepers of ancient traditions.

The polar regions hold many stunning sights such as the midnight sun and days of darkness caused by the high latitude. Much evidence of the last Ice Age, and the many lakes and rivers, evoke a feeling of ancient ties. Canada's north is a part of everyone in many ways and has much to offer.

ANADA'S MOST WESTERLY PROVINCE MAY ALSO BE THE most beautiful – it is no doubt the most varied in scenery. This is the home to the 440-metre Della Falls, the country's highest, and to the country's tallest and broadest trees. Considering the latter, it is no surprise to learn that BC also features the world's tallest totem pole, in Alert Bay, at a height of 52.7 metres. The world's highest (70 metres) and longest (137 metres) suspension foot bridge, the Capilano Suspension Bridge, is also a title BC holds. But it is mostly the varied scenery that draws people to live in and visit this place. With the most temperate climate of the country, BC is a perfect spot for all who enjoy skiing, surfing, scuba diving, whale watching and just plain good living.

Across the Strait of Georgia from mainland BC, on the absolute west coast of the country, is the largest island off the Pacific side of the continent – Vancouver Island. At 460 kilometres in length, and covered by the largest stand of timber in the world, Vancouver Island is a stunning place of fishing villages, beaches, mountains and rugged charm. With the mildest climate in the country, this is a major retirement centre and vacation spot. There are many opportunities for boating, surfing, hiking, fishing and camping all over the island. The capital of the province can be found on the south-eastern tip of the island. Victoria is a

wonderful, small city that is graced with English elegance, old-world charm and the fragrant beauty of flowers. In February, while most of Canada is still shovelling snow, the residents of Victoria take part in the annual flower count. Over five million blooms will be counted and enjoyed each early spring.

The focal point of this city is the Inner Harbour, which is faced by the grand Parliament Building, erected in 1897. This English-styled building features a massive dome on which a figure of Captain George Vancouver, the first British navigator to circle the island, stands. A gold statue of Queen Victoria, who chose the name of the province, can be found on the grounds that surround the popular structure. The distinct and refined Empress Hotel, built in 1905, is also in this area. The hotel is so renowned for its fancy tea service that it schedules three sittings for afternoon tea. For tea with different surroundings many visit the Upper Terrace at Crystal Gardens. The gardens feature an array of tropical plants, reptiles and exotic birds. Of course, Butchart Gardens feature the most famous gardens on the island with the popular Sunken Garden and Rose Garden. For beautiful sights of a different kind, the Emily Carr Gallery is dedicated to the works of Victoria's best-known painter.

British Columbia's Parliament Building, located in Victoria, is a stunning sight by night.

A whale frolics off the coast of Vancouver Island.

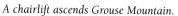

A chairlift ascends Grouse Mountain.

British Columbia's mainland offers scenery at its best. Half of the province is covered by productive forests. The eastern part of the province features the incredible Rocky Mountains, while southern BC is somewhat pastoral – the Okanagan Valley is known as the fruit basket of Canada. Sparkling lakes, attractive beaches, orchards and vineyards, along with a great amount of sun, make this a popular tourist destination. Golf, tennis, swimming, fishing and hiking are all centred around the main city in this series of valleys – Kelowna. Closer to the western part of the province, not far from Vancouver, are the mountains of Blackcomb, Whistler and Grouse. All three are popular ski spots and excellent summer resorts as well.

Capilano Suspension Bridge.

British Columbia offers some of the most varied and beautiful scenes in the country, such as this aerial view of Kicking Horse River.

Aerial view of Vancouver's waterfront featuring Canada Place.

With the sparkling waters of English Bay on three sides of this city, and the majestic mountains as a backdrop, Vancouver, the province's largest city, is beyond beautiful. The city's natural harbour is the busiest on the west coast of the continent. Canada Place, with its white simulated sails, resembles an ocean liner and adds to an already picturesque scene. Built to coincide with Expo '86, it is now home to the World Trade Centre, Vancouver Trade and Convention Centre, a hotel, shops, restaurants and the CN IMAX Theatre. Many special events take place here, as well as at GM Place and BC Place.

Pacific Rim National Park, Vancouver Island.

The city's Stanley Park, on a peninsula in English Bay, is a 400-hectare green area and a favourite place for locals and visitors alike. There's something for everyone with sports fields, trails, hills, beaches and plenty of parkland. The Vancouver Aquarium is in Stanley Park and features many wonders in water such as dolphins, sharks and even killer and beluga whales. Downtown, Robson Square is known as the city centre, which makes up three blocks of offices, restaurants, shops and theatres. The Vancouver Art Gallery is housed here, in an old courthouse. Downtown also features the country's largest Chinese community, centred around Pender Street. Gastown, a cobble-stoned street district, is the location of the city's beginnings and features the world's first steam-powered clock, which still whistles the hour to passersby. But it seems many people in this province of plenty do not need to know the time – they appear laid back and content to drink in the beauty that surrounds them.

The world's first steam-powered clock is located in Vancouver's Gastown area.

Skyline of Edmonton, the provincial capital of Alberta.

ALBERTA

CANADA'S PROVINCE OF ALBERTA IS THE 'WILD WEST' of the country, with a wide variety of features from large, modern cities to open fields, mines, rocky mountains and badlands. The province features two of the country's largest cities. Edmonton, the provincial capital, is known as the 'Oil Capital of Canada,' and is also home to the world's largest mall. In keeping with the 'large'

Night view of Calgary featuring the Saddledome and Calgary Tower.

theme in the province's largest city, the Edmonton Space and Science Centre features the largest planetarium in the country.

Calgary, another of Canada's large cities, has grown up between the flat farmlands and the foothills of the Rocky Mountains. Pictures of this city almost always feature the city's beloved Calgary Tower. It is a downtown landmark and symbol, but it is also appreciated for its revolving restaurant, observation deck and cocktail lounge. Also downtown is the country's longest-running noontime theatre, appropriately named the Lunchbox Theatre. Calgary is a city of head offices, a university and professional sport franchises. The Saddledome is where the National Hockey League's Calgary Flames play. The most exciting games are the ones played against their rivals, the Edmonton Oilers. Of course, Calgary is world famous for the 'Greatest Outdoor Show on Earth' – the Calgary Stampede. This annual event has been a popular one since its beginning in 1912. While there are a dizzying number of attractions and shows, the rodeo remains the best loved. The 15th Winter Olympics were hosted here in 1988. Many of the facilities already existed, while others were built especially for the games. A trip to the site reveals the unnerving height of the ski jumps and the steep bobsled and luge runs.

(above)
*The sharp contrast
between the plains and
mountains provides
a beauty unique to the
province of Alberta.*

(left)
Prehistoric Park, Calgary.

*The Banff Springs Hotel sits majestically amid snow covered
trees and mountains.*

Alberta has much to offer aside from its great cities. The badlands contain the world's largest discovery of dinosaur bones. Also in this arid desert area are the eerie, eroded columns of sandstone known as hoodoos. In the south is the oldest and biggest buffalo-jump site in North America. The well-preserved Head-Smashed-In Buffalo Jump, 18 kilometres from Fort McLeod, is a UN World Heritage Site. The Blackfoot Indians used to run bison over a cliff to kill them for food and other supplies. As legend has it, the name of the site is derived from the incident in which a young member of the community wished to view a killing from below, but was crushed by the falling bison. As well, the province is well known for its share of the magnificent Rocky Mountains. The largest mountain parkland in the world begins just 100 kilometres from Calgary. The skiing and climbing in Banff National Park are world famous and the larger and wilder Jasper National Park offers excellent hiking trails and wilderness experiences.

Alberta is both beautiful and unique in countless ways. It is the province with more sunshine than any other and while winters can be brutally cold, the dry, warm winds of the chinooks from the west offer yet more variety and pleasure to an already exciting part of Canada.

The Calgary Tower is a much-loved city landmark.

THE PROVINCE OF SASKATCHEWAN IS SYNONYMOUS WITH wheat, and with good reason. It is the greatest grower of wheat not only in Canada, but in North America. Describing this prairie province as flat and vast is completely accurate. Over one third of the country's farmland is here. The farmland meets the sky and the only significant skyline view is one with grain elevators and storage houses. But this is far from monotonous – it is a beautiful view of open space, huge skies, rolling cloud formations and, at the end of the day, stunning sunsets.

The calming flatness of the golden fields give way to the province's capital city of Regina. Adding yet more variety is Wascana Creek, which runs through this commercial, industrial and financial centre. This is a city of many parks, the largest of which is Wascana Centre. The 1,000-hectare area is the dominant feature in the city and aside from the beautiful parkland and artificial Wascana Lake, it is also one of the few places in the province that has trees (each one planted by hand). The park

is also home to many of the city's attractions such as the Saskatchewan Science Centre, which interestingly is housed in an overhauled power plant. Moved from its original location, the boyhood home of former Prime Minister John Diefenbaker can also be found here, as can

the Museum of Natural History, the Royal Saskatchewan Museum and the Provincial Legislative Building.

Saskatoon is a small city right in the middle of the prairies. It is not only a farm trading centre and home to an agricultural research centre, but something of a cultural centre for the province as well as a university town. The most exciting attraction in this area, Wanuskewin Heritage Park, is just north of Saskatoon. Here the story of the once buffalo-filled prairies is told. The 100-hectare site is centred around the scenic variety of the Opamihaw Valley, which is rich in Northern Plains Indian culture and prehistory. There are more than 20 prehistoric sites unearthed and archaeological digs are still active and accessible to the public. This magical valley is almost undetectable from the surrounding flat lands. Paths leading down into the valley are abundant with flora and fauna – it is truly a beautiful place. The name Wanuskewin means 'seeking peace of mind,' which is very fitting considering the paradise-like and ancient place that it is.

While Saskatchewan is mainly flat, there is some variation from this prairie generalization. The Big Muddy Badlands in the south offer hot, hilly valleys and oddly shaped sandstone formations. Cypress Hills Provincial Park, on the border of southern Saskatchewan and Alberta,

The farmland of Saskatchewan gives way to the city of Regina and Wascana Lake.

is an area greatly different from the wheat fields of the north, with lakes, parkland and green hills. The onion-domed churches of Yorkton, in eastern Saskatchewan, offer a change from the symbolic grain elevator and a bit of insight into the Ukrainian culture that is found here. Saskatchewan, in the sunny, golden prairies, is a place to appreciate the open skies and character of Canada's midwest.

Winter on the prairies is often both challenging and beautiful.

MANITOBA

THIS PROVINCE IS, LIKE ITS COUNTRY, ONE OF CONTRASTS. As well, this is the only prairie province that is partly covered by the Canadian Shield – ancient rocks, hills and forested lake land. North America's only tantalum mine can be found at Bernie Lake in this area. As well, both English and French hold equal status in the legislature. One of the country's oldest French communities, St. Boniface, is a suburb of Winnipeg.

The provincial capital, Winnipeg, Canada's fourth-largest city, is actually the geographic centre of the country. But it is a city that feels like it belongs to western Canada, with the flat prairie lands already beginning east of the city and with grain handling remaining an important part of the economy. The city is not only ethnically diverse, hosting the world's largest ethnocultural festival each summer, but it is pleasantly and architecturally diverse as well.

The Legislative Building is one of the world's finest examples of neoclassical architecture. Made with rare limestone, it is also one of the most valuable buildings in North America. Nearby, the lovely Victorian-style Macdonald House was built in 1895 for the son of the country's first prime minister, John A. Macdonald. The Winnipeg Art Gallery, aside from housing an excellent collection of Inuit and other Canadian art, is a striking, angular building that is shaped like the prow of a ship. Another substantial display of architecture is a 20-block area known as the Exchange District, which features beautiful turn-of-the-century commercial buildings and warehouses.

This city has a great amount of history. The Museum of Man and Nature is a superb place to discover much of this history, as is The Forks. The Forks is a riverside park at the forks of the Red and Assiniboine rivers where much of the city's history took place and can be learned through an historic stroll along Riverwalk. Restaurants and shops are housed in redeveloped factories and stables. The city's largest park is Assiniboine Park, which aside from its natural beauty features an English garden, a 40-hectare zoo, a conservatory and a sculpture garden.

Just north of Winnipeg is the country's fifth-largest lake and the dominant geographical feature of Manitoba. Lake Winnipeg stretches far into the untouched parts of northern Canada. The southern part of the lake provides splendid recreation in the form of beaches, including sand dunes for people and wetlands for animals. There are many wonderful parks in the province. In the west is the popular and spectacularly beautiful Riding Mountain

Assiniboine Park, which is Winnipeg's largest park, features a sculpture garden.

The Forks, seen here from Assiniboine River, is a popular riverside park.

The provincial Legislative Building, located in Winnipeg, boasts neoclassical architecture and limestone.

National Park, which is mostly highland and rises from the surrounding prairies in a 3,000-square-kilometre island.

Aside from the popular city of Winnipeg, far up north in the remote and forbidding part of the province where it snows for 10 months of the year, there is a small town that also draws international visitors. Churchill is one of the oldest parts of the country in terms of European exploration and was the first Hudson's Bay Company outpost site, set up in 1717. Today it is a small town with no luxuries, no trees, no traffic lights and only about 1,000 residents in the decline of grain handling. What makes this town interesting and worthy of international attention is that it sits right in the middle of a polar bear migration route, hence the title 'Polar Bear Capital of the World.' From late September to early November each year more than 150 polar bears pass through this town. Aside from these wildly beautiful and dangerous bears, beluga whales, seals (which are the polar bear's main source of meat), beaver, caribou and gray wolves are likely to be spotted. Manitoba, with its contrasts and varieties, literally has something for everyone.

ONTARIO

ONTARIO IS THE HUB OF THE COUNTRY AND FEATURES many attractions and tourist destinations. The country's largest city, Toronto, is here, as is Ottawa, the capital city of the country, and Niagara Falls, one of the country's top attractions. These elements make Ontario the most visited province in the country. There are many cities with various attractions, plus what's known as 'cottage country' in and around Lake Huron and Georgian Bay. Further north, wilderness parks are popular and resource-based cities such as Sudbury and Thunder Bay provide points of supply and information for the rugged northern parts of the province. As with much of the country there is a huge contrast between geography, environments, and therefore opportunities, in Ontario. One way to see much of the province is to drive the world's longest street. Yonge Street begins at Lake Ontario in Toronto and winds through the province for over 1,900 kilometres, north then west to the border of Manitoba.

Ottawa sits proudly on the south bank of the Ottawa River. Dominating the city is the stately Parliament Building on Parliament Hill. It is the most striking feature of the city, with its Peace Tower, clock and copper roofing on both sides. The inside is just as beautiful and equally interesting when the House of Commons and Senate can be viewed. During the summer months, the traditionally dressed Royal Canadian Mounted Police add yet another touch of pride to the scene. Most fittingly, the Supreme Court of Canada building, where the highest court in the land convenes, is architecturally intimidating. The entrance is a grand 12 metres high and is impressive in itself. The country's premier art gallery, the National Gallery, is another popular attraction in the capital. The building itself is impressive and inside displays a vast collection of international works. Many of the country's finest museums and galleries can be visited in Ottawa, including the National Aviation Museum, National Museum of Science and Technology, the Canadian Ski Museum and the Canadian Museum of Contemporary Photography.

The SkyDome and CN Tower are two of Ontario's best-known attractions.

The Governor General's Foot Guards march proudly in Ottawa, the nation's capital.

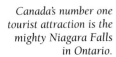

◀ July 1st marks Canada Day, which is cause for celebration across the country and on Parliament Hill in Ottawa.

Canada's number one tourist attraction is the mighty Niagara Falls in Ontario.

Reenactments by uniformed guards make a visit to Fort Henry a realistic trip to the past.

Ontario Place features a white geodesic dome known as the Cinesphere, where movies are shown on a six-storey-high circular screen.

*The Thousand Islands,
in eastern Ontario,
are actually made up
of nearly 2,000 islands.*

*The essence of Toronto,
the country's largest city,
is concentrated around the
historic and architecturally
stunning Union Station.*

*Nathan Phillips Square in Toronto
is the city hall's front yard and a
community gathering spot.*

Kingston, located about half way between Ottawa and Toronto, is somewhat of a historical city with many well-loved and preserved buildings. Just east of Kingston many visitors enjoy the beautiful Thousand Islands. In keeping with Kingston's historical reputation, a restored British fortification, Fort Henry, dominates the town from a hill-top on the outskirts. Dating from 1832, the beautiful structure is surrounded by uniformed guards who reenact military drills; displays go on throughout a visit.

With restored Fort York and many public historical homes and churches there is ample opportunity to continue an historical theme in Toronto. A favourite is Casa Loma, a 98-room Medieval-style castle built in the early 1900s. Toronto is also something of an arts centre for both the province and the country with musical bands, Broadway shows, dance and the fashion industry flourishing here. The Art Gallery of Ontario houses paintings from the 14th century to the present day and is well known for its vast collection of Henry Moore sculptures. The Royal Ontario Museum is Canada's largest museum and covers everything from the history of the human race to dinosaurs and Chinese crafts. The city has a multitude of attractions for both the tourist and local resident. Ontario Place, built offshore from the Canadian National Exhibition grounds on three artificial islands, is a popular spot for music, culture, rides and IMAX movies. The Ontario Science Centre also has many exciting exhibits for young and old.

Both the CN Tower, the world's tallest free-standing structure, and the SkyDome, where the beloved Toronto Blue Jays baseball team plays, are huge draws, but surprisingly another internationally known attraction is the city's Eaton Centre. Scores of shops and cafés are visited by thousands daily under an arched glass roof with designer geese suspended amid shiny decor, greenery, fountains and more. Just down the street, past the gorgeous Old City Hall, is Nathan Phillips Square, where the mayor of the mega-city makes big-city decisions. The courtyard in front is like a neighbourhood meeting place where many cultural events take place and the sparkling fountain waters turn into a public ice rink for the winter months. Just north of the city is a popular theme park – sort of a Canadian Disneyland. Paramount Canada's Wonderland features more than 50 rides, including some high-tech roller coasters, a huge water park, Hanna Barbera Land and live shows and concerts.

Aside from the many attractions, Toronto is a great place to visit and live because of its natural beauty and exciting multiculturalism. For a city that's home to close to three million people, Toronto is surprisingly clean and has many green areas and lush park land. Its many differing neighbourhoods, from Chinatown and Little Italy to Greek town, add a definite dash of internationalism to the mix.

Outside of Toronto, the main attraction in Ontario is most definitely Niagara Falls, but there are many small towns and cities with attractions, charm and nature of their own to offer residents and visitors. Picturesque scenes include farmland, Mennonite communities, Native reserves, canals, caves, orchards, forests and wetlands. Ontario as a whole is very popular with the outdoors type. Vacationing along Lakes Ontario, Erie and Huron is very popular and the landscape on Manitoulin Island, the world's largest freshwater island, is natural and rural. The provincial parks system is excellent and well used; boating, skiing, snow-mobiling and camping are at their best here. With most of the province's population living in the very southern portion of Ontario, the north is vast and thinly populated. Almost all life up here revolves around the natural resources of the forests, mines and lakes. Much of this portion of the province is uninhabited and wild.

While Ontario is home to the country's largest city as well as the nation's capital city, it is also a province of much farmland, wilderness and solitude.

CANADA'S LARGEST PROVINCE IS ONE OF MUCH WILDER-NESS, with 80 per cent covered by the Canadian Shield and two thirds by forest. The northern forests are coniferous, providing for a pulp and paper industry, the southern forests are deciduous, including the beloved maple tree. It is the maple tree that provides enough delicious maple syrup to make Quebec the world's largest producer of this sweet sauce – a truly Canadian treat on ice cream or pancakes. Much of the agriculture here takes place in the St. Lawrence Lowlands.

With so much wilderness it is not surprising that a great part of the province remains unspoiled and remote. The Gaspé Peninsula, southern Quebec's remotest area, has industry that consists mostly of fishing and forestry, but many crafters sell their works as well. In the town of Gaspé, where the first Canadian landing of Jacques Cartier took place in 1534, sailing and windsurfing on the Gulf of St. Lawrence are top notch. Nearby, the resort town of Percé is the busiest spot on the peninsula, where people enjoy watersports, fine hotel accommodation and the natural beauty and wonder of the cliffs that are pierced by the sea. Quebec's mountain range, the Laurentians, provides the best skiing in eastern Canada by winter and serves as a popular summer destination as well. Mont Tremblant, a major ski centre, boasts the highest peak in the Laurentians. Less than an hour's drive from the solitude of the Laurentians is Canada's second-largest city – Montreal.

Montreal is a fun city with friendly people, European flavour and an abundance of restaurants and nightlife. The world's second-largest French-speaking city after Paris, Montreal is alive with French culture, romance and charm. The city sits on an island, 40 kilometres long by 15 wide, where the Ottawa River travels into the St. Lawrence. Mount Royal, an extinct volcano in the middle of the island, affords the best view of the city at 232 metres above sea level. At the south end of Mount Royal Park is one of North America's most visited shrines; St. Joseph's Oratory attracts over two million pilgrims annually to pay homage to St. Joseph, patron saint of Canada. The basilica, whose copper dome is the second-largest in the world after St. Peter's in Rome, dominates the grand Italian Renaissance-style structure. Another popular church, in Old Montreal's Place d'Armes, is the Nôtre Dame Basilica, built in 1829. The Montreal Symphony Orchestra records and performs here along with many other famous musical organizations and individuals.

Montreal as seen from Mount Royal Park.

Old Montreal is the most beautiful, quaint and romantic part of the city, with cobble-stoned streets, artists and atmosphere galore. Place Jacques Cartier, which was originally opened as a marketplace back in 1804, is now the most popular Old City square with outdoor cafés, vendors and horse-drawn carriage tours. Of architectural interest is the imposing Bank of Montreal, built in 1847, with its striking Victorian exterior and opulent, marble-pillared interior. The Old Court House was built in the neoclassical style of the mid-19th century and Hôtel de Ville (City Hall) is a gorgeous structure and one of the most modern in Old Montreal even though it dates from 1878. The Saint-Sulpice Seminary, constructed in 1683, is the oldest structure.

Montreal's modern Olympic Stadium is easily recognized by its inclined tower.

Place Jacques Cartier, originally opened as a marketplace in 1804, is the most popular square in Old Montreal.

Beautiful St. Joseph's Oratory is imposing by night with its lighted cross and impressive shining dome.

South of Place Jacques Cartier is Old Port – where 100 berths and five container terminals spread along 25 kilometres of shoreline along with a waterfront district of tourist attractions. Also of interest to the tourist in Montreal is Olympic Park, featuring the famous Olympic Stadium with the world's tallest inclined tower at 175 metres. The Montreal Casino is a hot spot since its opening in 1993 and La Ronde, the city's amusement park, is located on Île Ste-Hélène. Montreal is also a city of arts and culture. Among the many worthy and famous galleries and museums is the world-renowned Musée des beaux arts (Fine Arts Museum). This is the city's main art gallery, with an extensive collection of more than 25,000 items. Quite fittingly, the Canadian Centre for Architecture is also located in Montreal.

The province's first casino, the Montreal Casino, was opened in 1993 in the modern French Pavilion from Expo '67.

Quebec City is an historic, romantic and charming city of many sights and sounds.

North of Montreal, Quebec City, the capital of Quebec, is one of the most visited destinations in the country and the heart of French Canada. The city sits on a cliff, Cap Diamant, overlooking the St. Lawrence River. It serves as a vital port and is dripping with enchanting history and charm. Most attractions are located in the old, walled city area – divided into Upper and Lower Towns. The entire section is a UN World Heritage Site.

The northeastern end of Upper Town is still surrounded by walls. These walls hold many treasured attractions, such as the stunning Basilica of Nôtre Dame. This beauty has endured a long history of bombardment, reconstruction and restoration but remains a powerful symbol of how strong a role the church plays in Quebec's history. The Ursuline Convent and Museum is the oldest girls' school on the continent. Among the many wondrous structures is some additional charm, with surprises like Rue du Trésor, leading from Place d'Armes, where artists gather to display their work, and the Latin Quarter with 18th-century homes, cafés and shops. The best-known landmark towers above Upper Town at the height of Cap Diamant. The castle-like Château Frontenac Hotel, built in 1892, is enchanting by day and night. Alongside the castle is the Dufferin Terrace, a perfect place to stroll and view the lovely St. Lawrence.

Rue de Petit Champlain is considered the oldest street in North America, dating back to the founding of the city in 1608.

The picturesque Château Frontenac Hotel has been a treasured landmark since it was built in 1892.

Winter falls upon Quebec City.

Percé Rock juts out of the St. Lawrence near the Gaspé Peninsula.

The province of Quebec holds the title as the world's largest producer of maple syrup.

Lower Town's focal point is Place Royale – a beautiful square with elegant 17th- and 18th-century houses. Old Port is the place to attend open-air concerts, theatre and craft markets. Outside of the walls, the star-shaped Citadel, built by the French in 1750, stands on the highest point overlooking the city. This old fort serves as a base to today's Royal 22s. The Changing of the Guard during summer months is popular with visitors. Running southwest from the Citadel is a pleasant, hilly, treed park known as Battlefields Park. Not always so peaceful, one particular section, known as the Plains of Abraham, is the site where the English defeated the French in 1759 – a battle that saw generals on both sides killed.

Outside of Quebec City, Mont Sainte-Anne is the largest ski resort in all of Quebec. The landmark Montmorency Falls are an amazing sight to behold year round. This spectacular display of nature plunges 84 metres by summer and almost totally freezes by winter. Six kilometres south of the waterfall is one of Quebec's most important religious sites – Ste-Anne de Beaupre. The community of Ste-Anne has been known as a religious site since 1658, when it's believed that the mother of the Virgin Mary saved the lives of sailors shipwrecked off nearby Cap Tourmenté.

Breathtaking Montmorency Falls.

Mont Sainte-Anne is the largest ski resort in Quebec, with over 40 challenging runs, and has a reputation for providing the best groomed ski trails in North America.

Halifax, with its much-loved Old Town Clock, is the capital of the province.

 # NOVA SCOTIA

THE MOST VISITED OF CANADA'S ATLANTIC PROVINCES offers scenic variety and beauty, history and character. A province in which you are never more than an hour from the sea, Nova Scotia offers everything from quaint fishing villages along the deeply indented coastline to rugged plateaus and gentle scenes of farmland. It was here that North America's first lighthouse was built in 1720 at Louisbourg. Today, Peggy's Cove, with its picturesque post office lighthouse, is one of the most popular tourist destinations on the continent and well known throughout the world. There is no other place like this – this is the Maritimes of Canada.

The largest city in Nova Scotia, Halifax is also the capital of the province and a principal port in Atlantic Canada. Harbourfront runs along the second-largest natural harbour in the world (after Sydney, Australia). Aside from the many boats and ships, this is a charming spot where old warehouses and wharves are classified as historic properties. These properties house trendy, high-quality galleries, shops and restaurants. Lunch on an open-air terrace accompanied by an ocean breeze, or an evening at the dockyard for live pub music, are two of the many opportunities here. The Maritime Museum of the Atlantic, also at Harbourfront, is housed in a turn-of-the-century ship chandlery. One of the many fantastic displays is an account of the Great

Explosion that took place off the shores of Halifax in 1945.

One of the city's most loved symbols is the Old Town Clock that sits distinctly on Citadel Hill. The Citadel National Historic Site is a towering landmark itself, with a huge, angled fort sitting atop the city's largest hill. The Army Museum can be visited here and the park is a popular one for viewing the city or relaxing in the sun.

The south shore of the province is where Canada's best-known fishing village, Peggy's Cove, can be found. There are many other picturesque scenes in this area as well, such as St. Margaret's Bay – a collection of small towns that seem dedicated to the arts and crafts and also boast many fine beaches. Lunenburg, best known for building the *Bluenose* sailing schooner in 1921, is a UN World Heritage Site. Apart from the Lunenburg Fisheries Museum and a major fleet in the harbour, this town offers some splendid and varied architecture. Yarmouth is the largest town in western Nova Scotia and boasts a major fishing port with rows of wharves, some for boats and others for entertainment. Up by Digby Neck, alongside a long, thin strip of land that juts into the Bay of Fundy, are Long and Barrier islands. Long Island is home to an odd attraction known as Balancing Rock, a seven-metre-high stone column that literally appears to be balanced on the edge of a cliff.

The fertile lands of the Annapolis Valley provide abundant crops.

Even though much of the province is not suitable for agriculture, the soil in and around the Annapolis Valley is as rich and fertile as can be. Farms and orchards create not only the most breathtaking country scenes, but wonderful crops. The pink and white blossoms of the apple orchards produce such delicious fruit that the valley is famous for its apples. The province is also appreciated for its culture. Pictou, on the Northumberland Shore, is where the Highland Scots first landed in 1773. Antigonish, a university and residential town, is known for the annual Highland Games. Gaelic and French can still be heard in the villages on Cape Breton Island. But it is the breathtaking scenery that makes this large island at the northeast end of the province popular. The rocky, sometimes steep coast climbs 500 metres between sea and mountain. The 300-kilometre Cabot Trail, around Cape Breton Highlands National Park, is one of the country's best-known roads. It winds and climbs through mountains, rivers, lakes and pure rugged splendour.

Cape Breton Highlands National Park features the country's best-known road, the winding and climbing Cabot Trail.

Peggy's Cove is Canada's best-known fishing village, drawing visitors from all around the world.

Lunenburg is typical of the many historic and scenic seaports and fishing villages dotting Nova Scotia's coastline.

The Halifax Public Gardens are an excellent example of a formal Victorian garden.

NEW BRUNSWICK IS WILD AND BEAUTIFUL, WITH A greater percentage of forest cover than any other province in the country. A variety of geography, including uplands, rolling hills and lowland plain, makes this area a diverse pleasure. Rushing rivers, sparkling streams, several natural harbours, fertile river valleys, fisheries and mineral deposits make New Brunswick a land of natural resources. This is the largest potato-producing area in the country and is also the covered bridge capital of Canada, with over 70 of the charming structures. The world's longest covered bridge, at 390 metres, spans the Saint John River at Hartland. There are many prime locations for whale watching around the provincial coast as well. The culture is rich, with a strong Acadian influence; the largest Danish community in North America resides in New Denmark. Unique, natural and charming, New Brunswick has much to offer.

Fredericton, the capital of the province, is a pretty city that features a number of attractions, including a very large frog. This famous frog is a sort of beloved mascot for the town. The 19-kilogram pet is now in a glass case at the York-Sunbury Museum, but first appeared, at 3.6 kilograms, on the boat of a local inn keeper, Fred Coleman, in 1885. Coleman fed the frog until it became the world's largest. Today, Coleman Frog T-shirts are a popular item in this area. Aside from the frog, the Officer's Square, the city's central park, is a popular spot and was once the site of a military parade ground. Outside of Fredericton, Gagetown is a charming village on the banks of Gagetown Creek. One of the oldest English settlements in the area, Gagetown is an artist's haven today, featuring pottery shops, galleries and the like.

The name Saint John is never abbreviated so as to avoid confusion with the capital of Newfoundland – St. John's. Saint John, which sits at the mouth of the St. John River, is the oldest incorporated city in the country. But it is probably best known for its Moosehead Beer and Reversing

Quoddy Head Lighthouse.

The magnificent sea-carved rocks of Hopewell Cape draw thousands of visitors to New Brunswick each year.

Stretching 390 metres (1,282 feet) across the St. John River, the Hartland Covered Bridge is the longest covered bridge in the world.

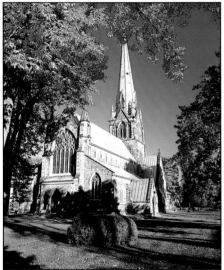

Considered both a spectacular event and natural phenomenon, the waters at the foot of the St. John River reverse direction during tidal changes.

Fredericton, the provincial capital, offers many pretty scenes.

Falls. When the Bay of Fundy tides rise, the current in the river reverses, causing the water to flow upstream. When the tide goes back down the water flows in the natural direction again. The Moosehead Brewery in town is the largest Canadian-owned brewery and Canada's oldest independent beer maker, dating back to 1867.

The city of Moncton is the major transportation and distribution centre for the Atlantic provinces. There are also some attractions in this area. Magnetic Hill is a site where a car or bike at the bottom of a hill will drift upward. The Rocks Provincial Park features unusual erosions from the great tides. It is a great experience to walk among these 'rocks' on the wet sandy bottom when the tide is out. Fundy National Park is one of the country's most popular parks and the place to witness the world's highest tides. Because of the length, depths and funnel shapes of the Bay of Fundy, the southern edge of the province has constantly rising and falling tides from the bay. New Brunswick recently has been linked with its maritime neighbour, Prince Edward Island, by way of an architectural feat – the Confederation Bridge. The longest bridge over ice-covered waters in the world begins at Cape Jourimain, New Brunswick.

The senses and logic of tourists are challenged at Magnetic Hill in Moncton.

PRINCE EDWARD ISLAND

Spanning 12.9 kilometres from the province of New Brunswick, the Confederation Bridge stretches to Borden-Carleton on 'the Island.' Opened on May 31, 1997, this masterpiece brings a new age of transportation to Atlantic Canada. What used to be a lengthy event including line ups, parking and ferrying across to Prince Edward Island is now a 10-minute car ride across a two-lane bridge any time of the day or night. The bridge has meant a change in the way of life for residents of the smallest province in the country. Many more people are venturing across to take in the peaceful, fresh, pastoral hills and sparkling harbours of PEI. For such a small place, the province is well known for much of its character, including the delicious lobster, the potato (which is sold all across the country), the distinctive red soil and a world-famous red head – Anne of Green Gables.

If left unpicked lupins, which can grow up to 60 centimetres tall, tend to multiply, covering a larger area each year.

Lucy Maud Montgomery, the author of the 1908 novel *Anne of Green Gables*, was born in New London, PEI. Her novel is set in Cavendish, where Green Gables House and the surrounding lands also described in the novel can be visited today. The entire island seems to have an Anne theme for visitors to enjoy. Much of the island is still as green and enchanting as Montgomery described it almost a century ago.

The capital city of Charlottetown, while modern for the most part, retains its small-town look and feel. Province House, a neo-classical sandstone building, is a National Historic Site in downtown Charlottetown. It was here that the fathers of Confederation met in a room on the second floor in 1864. The room remains as it would have been during the work on creating the Dominion of Canada. The beautiful structure, originally a courthouse, is also the current Provincial Legislature. The Confederation Centre for the Arts adds drastic contrast to the downtown with a large modern exterior. Inside, a museum, art gallery, library and theatre are housed.

'The Island,' as it's affectionately called by most residents, offers many peaceful settings and scenes. There are many small harbours and plenty of opportunities to partake in the famous lobster suppers – broiled, barbecued, baked or boiled, these suppers live up to their reputation. Purple lupins are another pleasure as they are plentiful in this land. Cavendish offers some typical tourist attractions, with rides and restaurants, as a means to draw the Green Gables visitors. Also here is one of the island's most popular beaches. Cavendish Beach features a wide expanse of sand, huge sand dunes and rocky cliffs. Victoria is a picturesque fishing village where many artists can be found along with their studios and galleries. A Victorian Lighthouse here is now a one-room museum and the wharf is lined with quaint shops and tempting restaurants. Summerside, the second-largest city in the province, is home to the College of Piping and Celtic Performing Arts, which makes for some fine entertainment. There is also a mid-summer Lobster Carnival here as well. For those who prefer the ferry as a means to visit or depart this wonderful island, the Northumberland Ferries between Wood Islands, PEI, and Caribou, NS, still chug across Northumberland Strait.

This famous farmhouse is the setting that inspired PEI-born author Lucy Maud Montgomery to write the cherished Anne of Green Gables novel published in 1908.

Quaint and charming Charlottetown serves as the province's capital.

Prince Edward Island National Park offers 40 kilometres of beaches, which include popular Cavendish Beach.

Rustico Bay is one of the oldest established areas in the province.

NORTH AMERICA'S FOURTH-LARGEST ISLAND IS ALSO the most distinctive and interesting. Labrador (located on the mainland northeast of Quebec) and the northern parts of the island are part of the Laurentian Shield, one of the earliest geological formations on earth. The interior portion of the island is well forested, while the southern coastal plain is barren and rugged.

Most residents of this province live along the Avalon Peninsula. This area is rich with history and breathtaking coastal scenery. Conception Bay is lined with small communities and fishing villages. Argentia, on the southwest portion of the peninsula, is where the ferry crosses to Nova Scotia. St. John's is the capital city of the province and the most easterly city in Canada. This warm and friendly place is also the oldest city in North America. Rising from the waterfront, stairs, steep streets, alleys and hills wind through pastel-coloured clapboard houses. There are many churches in town, including the Basilica of St. John the Baptist, built in 1855, which dominates the city with its Gothic facade.

The best view of St. John's is from Signal Hill National Historic Park. At the top of the hill, the Cabot Tower honours John Cabot's arrival in 1497. This is also the tower where Marconi received the first wireless transatlantic message in 1901, sent from Cornwall, England. On the northwest edge of the city, CA Pippy Park features a number of attractions, including recreations facilities, picnic areas, wildlife, Memorial University and the Newfoundland Freshwater Resource Centre. The centre features the only public fluvarium in North America. Visitors can observe the natural and undisturbed life beneath the surface of Nagle's Hill Brook behind a 25-metre glass wall.

Just south of St. John's is Petty Harbour. A very scenic harbour complete with weathered boats and docks, it is surrounded by the rocky hills of Newfoundland and is often used in movie productions because of its typical beauty. Over Signal Hill is Quidi Vidi, a tiny picturesque village and fishing port. It is home to the oldest cottage in North America. Mallard Cottage was built in the early 1700s and is now a National Heritage Site and gift shop. Quidi Vidi Lake is the site of the annual Royal St. John's Regatta, which has taken place since 1826.

Cape Spear features nature trails that lead visitors past the most easterly point in North America. The scenery here is more than spectacular and includes everything from whales to icebergs, which can be as tall as five storeys – and that's only the part that shows above water. The origin of these frosty giants is Greenland, where glaciers produce up to 40,000 icebergs each year. The entire region of Cape Spear is preserved as a National Historic Site complete with an 1835 lighthouse, which now serves as an interpretive centre.

St. John's, the capital of the province, is the oldest city in North America.

Quidi Vidi Village is a picturesque fishing port.

Signal Hill National Historic Park features the Cabot Tower and offers a spectacular view of St. John's.

The always-impressive humpback whale.

On the west side of the island, Corner Brook is the second-largest town in the province. This is the sunniest region and has some interesting sites. For an excellent view of the city, visitors head up to the cliffs overlooking the Humber Arm. A National Historic Site, here Captain James Cook is honoured with a monument for his work surveying the region in the mid 1760s. Up north, L'Anse-aux-Meadows National Historic Park is a 1,000-year-old Viking settlement. The park remains much like it was when the Scandinavian and Greenland Vikings arrived. They were the first Europeans to land in North America. Across the Strait of Belle Isle is one of the largest, cleanest and most natural regions in the country – Labrador. It is home to the world's largest herd of caribou and, until recently, the only human residents included the Inuit and a few long-time residents decended from early European settlers.

'The Rock,' as Newfoundland is known, is a unique place with much beauty, history and character. Aside from the varied land, the people of Newfoundland are an interesting group, mainly of English and Irish descent; they've developed their own distinct culture. Of particular interest is the definite dialect, slang and inflections of their language. Although they're speaking English, even fellow Canadians sometimes cannot understand them. Newfoundlanders are friendly people with a wit that has developed from the hardship and realities of living in a unique and challenging environment.

◄ *Up to 800 giant white icebergs make their way south along the coast of Newfoundland each year.*

After floating on the ocean and diving for fish during the winter, puffins come ashore by the hundreds in the spring to begin courting.

SEASONS

CANADA'S SEASONS FOLLOW THE THEME OF CONTRAST, challenge and beauty that the country portrays through all of its features. If variety is the spice of life, then Canadians are the most alive people on the globe. There are four distinctly different seasons across the country, arriving at varying times and with differing degrees of impact from province to province. Summer days may be sweltering in any part of the country, springs are sometimes violent and wet, other times playing out with snow and wind and yet many times dry and renewing. Autumn brings with it an almost spiritual winding down – the leaves change colour and provide a vibrant display of multitudinous colour and drama before winter falls upon the country. Some parts of the country receive snowfalls only three or four times a season. But most parts may see as much in an afternoon.

It is winter that reminds Canadians that they live in a land of both splendid luxuries and harsh realities. It is this mixture that shapes the personality of Canada and its people. The many contrasts in geography, people and cultures are reflected in the variety of seasons this country offers. The combination of the many characteristics Canada holds as a country is both dramatic and beautiful in countless ways.

Published and Distributed by

Irving Weisdorf & Co. Ltd.

2801 John Street,
Markham, Ontario L3R 2Y8

Writer/Photo Editor	Art Director/Designer	Designer/Typesetter
Sandra Tonn	**Nebosja Stojkovic**	**Arlene Cheel**

Photography by:

Barrett and Mackay	26a, 26b, 88b, 89a, 92, 93d	Nick Newbery	8, 35b, 64/65, 65a
Bill Walker	51d	Palmer Publicity Ink, Ltd.	
Birds Eye View Photo		Andrew Eccles	42b
Ron Garnett	91a, 93a	Paul Hartley	6/7, 10c, 32b, 32d
Bob Evans	84c	Paul Heppner	28b
Cameras North	4a, 60a, 60c	Ron Garnett	front cover d, 3a, 6, 29, 33,
The Postcard Factory	35d, 38b, 39b, 40b, 50b, 77a,		66/67, 68a, 70d, 87b, 90/91,
	77b, 78c, 79a, 83a, 83c, 85b,		90b, 91b
	94a, 94b, 94c, 95c, 95e, 95g	Terry Parker	7, 35g, 63b, 63c
Comstock Stock Photography	93e	The Postcard Factory	4h, 5c, 5e, 13, 14/15, 18, 19b,
Craig Hamm	38a		19c, 20a, 20b, 21a, 21b, 21c,
Don Johnson	48d		21d, 22, 22/23, 23, 34a, 34b,
First Light			35e, 35f, 36b, 39d, 44b, 44c,
Michio Hoshino	4b, 62/63		46b, 48a, 54a, 54c, 58/59, 66,
Gerard Romany	5b, 5d, 37a, 39c, 53b, 55a,		68c, 68d, 75d, 78/79, 78a, 79b,
	78b, 84b, 86, 87e, 89d, 91c,		80a, 80b, 80c, 82b, 84d, 87a,
	93f, 93c, 94d, back cover b		87c, 88a, 89b, 89c, 90a, 95b,
Hot Shots Stock Shots			95d, 95f, back cover e f
Chris Junck	49b	Tony Stone Images	
Janina W. Swietlik	65b	Arnulf Husmo	back cover a
Kaj Svensson	32b, 41a, 47a, 47b,	Valan Photos	title page
Larry Fisher	front cover a b c e, 3b, 4d,	Wally Hayes	87d
	4e, 10b, 16/17, 19a, 24a, 24c,		
	25, 27, 28a, 32a, 36c, 37b,		
	40c, 42d, 43a, 48b, 54/55,	**Additional Photography Courtesy of**	
	54b, 55b, 67a, 67b, 67c,	Butchart Gardens Ltd. – 24b	
	67d, 69a, 69b, 70b, 70c, 71,	City of Toronto Archives – 10a	
	75a, 75c, 77c, 81, 82a, 82c,	CN Tower – 17a, 17b	
	82d, 83b, 84a	House of Commons/Government of Canada – 52	
Malak Photographs Limited	9, 41b, 60b, 61, 63a, 91d	Jean Sylvain/Mont-Sainte-Anne – 5a, 35a, 46a, 85a, 85c	
Masterfile		Kitchener-Waterloo Oktoberfest – 38c	
Bill Brooks	12/13	Lydia Paweiak/National Ballet of Canada – 43b	
J.A. Kraulis	30	Maurice Wong/Dragon Boat Festival – 36a	
Janet Foster	2/3	Michael Burns Photography/The Ontario Jockey Club – 38d	
Larry Fisher	2	Nancy Richardson School of Highland Dancing – 39a	
McMichael Canadian Art Collection	40a, 41c	National Capital Commission – 53a, 57a, 76, 95a	
Mike Grandmaison	4f, 4g, 35c, 42a, 49a, 50a, 51a,	Photo Library of the National Film Board of Canada	
	70a, 72, 72/73, 73a, 74, 75b	© National Film Board of Canada – 42c, 48c (*All Rights Reserved*)	
Mike R. Byneshewsky	73b, back cover c	RCMP Museum, Regina, Saskatchewan – 56, 57b, back cover d	
National Archives of Canada		Robin Leworthy/Ontario Lacrosse – 46c	
Gazette Collection	11a	Toronto Blue Jays Baseball Club – 45a	
Notman and Son Ltd.	11b	Vancouver Trade and Convention Centre – 68b	
National Film Board of Canada	53c	Vineland Estates – 51b, 51c	
NBA Photos		Pete Neilson/Wildwoods Expeditions – 4c	
Andy Hayt	45b		
NHL Images			
Mitchell Layton	44a		

Printed in Korea